T5-BQB-564

International Joint Venture Formation in the Agribusiness Sector

The case of sub-Saharan African countries

HABTE GEBRE SELASSIE
Department of Marketing and Business Management
Cranfield University
Silsoe College

Ashgate

Aldershot • Brookfield USA • Singapore • Sydney

© H .G. Selassie 1995

All rights reserved. No part of this publication may be reproduced, stored in a retrieval system, or transmitted in any form or by any means, electronic, mechanical, photocopying, recording or otherwise without the prior permission of the publisher.

Published by
Ashgate Publishing Ltd
Gower House
Croft Road
Aldershot
Hants. GU11 3HR
England

HD
9017
.A2
H33
1995

Ashgate Publishing Company
Old Post Road
Brookfield
Vermont 05036
USA

British Library Cataloguing in Publication Data

Selassie, Habte Gebre
  International Joint Venture Formation in
  the Agribusiness Sector: Case of
  Sub-Saharan African Countries. - (Making of
  Modern Africa Series)
  I. Title II. Series
  338.967

ISBN 1 85628 993 1

Library of Congress Catalog Card Number: 94-73135

Reprinted 1998

Printed in Great Britain by Biddles Limited, Guildford and King's Lynn

INTERNATIONAL JOINT VENTURE FORMATION IN THE AGRIBUSINESS SECTOR

Contents

v

Tables and figures

ix

Note about the author

Habte G Selassie is Lecturer in Marketing, the Department of Marketing and Business Management, Silsoe College, Cranfield University, Bedford, UK. He lectures on marketing research, data analysis and interpretation, and international business collaborations, and specializes in marketing systems in developing countries.

His research interests include international joint ventures, market liberalization and privatization policies in developing countries, and promotion of small businesses in developing countries. Dr Selassie has accumulated a considerable research and practical experiences in marketing, agribusiness management, and regional development planning and evaluation in developing countries context, with frequent travels to African and Middle Eastern countries.

Acknowledgments

This book is based on my PhD thesis. The undertaking of the thesis over a period of more than 3 years required field work and systematic data collection in two countries, the UK and Zimbabwe; and discussions with people of various stature: company executives, officials of government departments, international organizations and private institutions, university lecturers and friends. I am grateful to all these people who shared their time, valuable information and provided advice.

I am greatly indebted to Professor Roy Hill, my research supervisor, for his guidance and encouragement not only during the research period but later as well during the preparation of this manuscript for publication. I would like to thank Mr Ian Crawford for his assistance and critical comments particularly on methodology and statistical techniques applied in the study. Assistance was given by a large number of people at Silsoe College, and the School of Management, Cranfield University. I am particularly grateful to Dr J. Morris, Mr Tim Harding, Mr C. Marshal, Dr S. Vyakarnam, and also to the staff of the libraries at Silsoe College and at the School of Management. My thanks also go to the secretaries of the Marketing and Business Management Department, Mrs Carol Clarke, Mrs Linda Chapman and Mrs Lena Holmes for their help.

Part of the field work was carried out in Zimbabwe. I owe the success of the field work in Zimbabwe to a number of people, foremost to Dr J. Meadley. Besides his valuable comments and interest in the study, he helped in arranging a place of work in Harare and provided important contacts. While in Zimbabwe, EDESA Ltd. provided me with an office with the facilities I required to conduct my research. I would like to express my gratitude to the management and staff of EDESA. Dr Steve Carter of FAO, Mr Ruphael Arega of the Ethiopian Embassy and Dr Asrat Tsegaye of the

University of Zimbabwe helped me in contacting relevant people and organizations, and made my stay in Harare not only fruitful but enjoyable as well.

Finally, I would like to mention that while many people have assisted me in the completion of this study, any errors or faults that may occur remain mine alone.

Abbreviations

DCs	developing countries
ESACs	English-speaking African countries
FDI	Foreign direct investment
JV	joint ventures
MNC	multinational corporation
NFI	New forms of investment
TNC	transnational corporation
ESAP	economic structural adjustment program
SSACs	sub-Saharan African countries
wos	wholly-owned subsidiaries

1 Introduction

Background

Agriculture provides the livelihood for the majority of the population in sub-Saharan African countries (SSACs) (1). Agriculture accounts for about 40% of the GDP, 75% of employment and 40% of exports (World Bank, 1988). The percentage of agricultural exports is much higher in most countries than the 40% figure suggests (e.g. Ethiopia 97%, Kenya 70%, Tanzania 79%, Zimbabwe 41%). Agriculture is the basis of industrial development, as agro-processing accounts for about 50% of the manufacturing value added (UNIDO 1989).

The vital role of agro-processing in reversing the problem of low foreign currency earnings in particular, and breaking the basic constraints of development in general is strongly stressed in the literature. Thus, it becomes apparent that economic development and higher standard of living for the population in Africa is closely linked to improvements in the agribusiness sector.

The problems in bringing about development in African countries have been the lack of technology, capital and various skills. Joint ventures (JVs) are considered as one of the mechanisms for tackling these problems, and on the whole, JVs have grown popular not only in the developing countries (DCs) but in the economically advanced countries as well. However, there is doubt as to whether African countries have succeeded in attracting foreign firms for partnership in JVs as the following evidences show:

i)   Foreign investment, of which JVs are a part, has been declining as a percentage of GDP in Africa: from 20% in the 1970's to 15% in the

1980's (the Economist, 1989). Besides, the flow of foreign direct investment to African countries has been concentrating in only a few oil exporting countries. A United Nations report (UNCTC 1988) indicated that during the period 1981-1985, 5 countries (Algeria, Cameroon, Egypt, Nigeria and Tunisia) accounted for 90% of the foreign direct investment inflows to Africa. This situation, coupled with the low domestic investment and capital formation, and the debt burden has been a serious problem. Therefore, as pointed out by Bennell (1990) the question for SSACs is not whether they need foreign investment but whether they can attract sufficient investment to impact positively on development.

ii)   Some authors (e.g., Stoever 1989) indicate that many DC governments have not been successful in attracting foreign investment, including JVs. According to Stoever, policy makers in DCs lack marketing orientation and fail to satisfy the concerns of the foreign companies. He, therefore, suggested undertaking marketing research into what is likely to motivate a foreign company's decision to invest in a particular DC.

iii)   There is little mention in the literature of the role of JVs in SSACs, which is an indication by itself that JVs have not yet had significant impact in the economy so far. A review of the literature on JVs indicates that the focus of research and general interest has been placed on partnerships between firms of the industrialized countries, between firms of Western and Eastern European countries; and to some extent between firms of the industrialized countries and those of the DCs of Latin America, Asia and the Middle East, with little attention to the sub-Saharan African region.

The literature indicates that the 'divorce rate' or failure of JVs has been relatively high. Though the major reasons mentioned are 'post formation' problems, such as lack of commitment by partners, government interventions, conflict in management and control, there are evidences to show that most problems originate from the 'creation' or formation stage. (Simiar 1983). Therefore, understanding the motives of both foreign firms and host firms in a JV, and identifying the problems that inhibit the achievement of their respective objectives will contribute towards starting more successful JVs.

2

This study is in part a response to the above stated concerns. The research question is, therefore, what factors determine the formation of JVs in the food and agribusiness sector in SSACs between foreign firms and local host firms, and what can be done to promote such JVs in the food and agribusiness sector of SSACs.

Objectives of the study

The aim of the study is to identify and assess some of the major factors that determine the formation of JVs in the agribusiness sector in the countries of sub-Saharan Africa, and to propose ways of attracting more foreign firms as partners. The specific objectives of the study are outlined as follows:

i)   To compile a framework for defining and classifying JVs in the African context. This is done through a critical review of various definitions provided in the literature. Various JVs in SSACs are reviewed and a working definition is proposed.

ii)   To explain the reasons for JV formation in general. An attempt is made to answer why firms (both foreign and host) go for JVs. Explanation is also sought for why joint venturing has grown popular.

iii) To examine the JV entry environment in a selected African country. Specifically, an answer is sought for the question: what are the entry conditions for JV formation in terms of opportunities for JVs in agribusiness sector, types and capabilities of host firms as JV partners, effectiveness of current policies and organizations promoting JVs, and the general attitudes towards joint venturing in the host country.

iv)   To determine which forms of market entry mode are preferred by foreign firms with regard to SSACs. For a company, the spectrum of entry to a foreign market ranges from 'export' to 'foreign production', each associated to a certain level of risk, and control over strategy (Cundiff & Hilger 1988, Cavusgil & Ghauri 1990). Though it can be assumed that wholly-owned subsidiaries (wos), JVs and licensing represent the major forms of investment,

3

management and technical contracts can also be considered, and placed on the continuum.

v)   To determine the preferences of foreign firms as regards to the types of host partners (state, private, public, and others). Many studies indicate that foreign firms avoid state-owned firms in host countries as partners. On the other hand, for various obvious reasons state-owned firms come up as prospective partners.

vi)   To determine the most important (critical) resources sought by foreign firms from host partners. As the basis for all JVs is exchange of resources between partners, the availability of resources and attributes sought by foreign firms from prospective host partners is an important factor.

vii)   To identify host country specific factors that are perceived as barriers to enter SSACs for JV formation. Major factors are identified through literature review and verified further by a pilot study. These factors are further examined rigorously with a larger number of respondents to identify those which are more critical and thus could be barriers to JV formation.

viii) To find out if large foreign firms and medium/small foreign firms differ in their attitudes towards JV formation in SSACs particularly with regard to the variables outlined in the objectives iv to vii. More specifically, the study attempts to find out whether large firms and medium/small firms differ in: a) their preferences to the different modes of market entry, b) their preferences to the different types of host partners, c) in the type of resources and attributes they seek from prospective host partners, and d) in their evaluation of the host-country specific factors as barriers to enter into JVs in SSACs.

ix)   To identify and recommend guidelines for policy and support systems for the promotion of joint agribusiness ventures in SSACs.

Significance of the study

There are four major reasons why this study is significant, which are discussed briefly in the following paragraphs.

Agribusiness

The book deals with the food and agribusiness sector with regards to SSACs, and this is considered important in two major aspects: empirical and theoretical. Empirically, agribusiness in general and the food sector in particular is the basis for the economic and social development in SSACs; and tackling issues that inhibit this development are timely and very important for the following reasons:

i)   Besides being the largest contributor to GDP in many SSACs as already shown, agribusiness is also the sector with the greatest potential to attract foreign investors. For instance, in Mauritania, a country with scarce resources even by African standards, abundant fish resources are indicated as an area of great opportunity for joint venturing with foreign firms.(Tuttle & Buchmiller 1988). In Nigeria, Ghana, Senegal, Liberia, Cameroon and in many other countries agribusiness in general, and food processing in particular are the foremost areas of business opportunities for foreign investment.(Onah 1989, Fieldman 1987).

ii)   Food output in SSACs has not increased in the past few decades. In fact, dependence of the countries of the region on imported food has increased (Dinham & Hines 1983, Baum & Tolbert 1985). With the objective of food self-sufficiency and enhancing foreign currency earnings, governments of SSACs have drawn up policies with special attention to the agribusiness sector. Therefore this study, albeit with a modest impact, will contribute to tackle issues and problems of an area of high priority for development in SSACs.

iii)   SSACs are faced with an increasingly competitive environment in the international market place. The necessity for continuous innovation and upgrading of ones competitive advantage for a nation to be able to effectively compete in international markets is strongly stressed (e.g. Porter 1992).

Theoretically, the study has importance in two respects:

i)   Research on JVs in the generic form has focused on the manufacturing sector, and it is doubtful whether prior studies have

5

properly addressed the particular characteristics of agribusiness. Torok et al. (1991), for instance, question the relevance of generic aggregate business studies to specific industries. Baum & Tolbert, Downey and Erickson (1987), and Torok et al. have discussed the characteristics of agribusiness that differentiates it from other sectors, and therefore why agribusiness management is unique. The major ones are: a) high seasonality in agricultural production, b) agribusinesses are targets of direct government programs and policies, c) exposure to various vagaries of nature; d) their small size, e) raw products are the nucleus for their operation, and f) their family/community orientation.

ii)   Many previous studies of JVs characterized a foreign firm partner as an MNC (or a TNC). This study attempts to identify the possible differences in attitudes and propensities to enter into JVs in the agribusiness sector in SSACs by distinguishing between two sets of foreign firms: large firms and medium/small firms.

Population growth and urbanization

SSACs are among the regions of the world where population growth and urbanization are very high. Table 1.1 shows that sub-Saharan Africa has the highest rate of population growth. Even compared to the average population growth rates of the 'low- and middle-income countries' group, that of sub-Saharan Africa will be 72% higher by the year 2000. The expected population growth in general and the growing number of the labor force in particular are described as 'alarming'. (Loutfi).

Baum & Tolbert point out that the rate of urbanization in Africa has also been higher than in other low-income and middle-income regions. Therefore, creating employment opportunities and producing enough food for the growing population and urbanization are among the current challenges policy makers in SSACs are facing.

Declining foreign investment

The flow of foreign investment to countries of sub-Saharan Africa has been declining over the past two decades. A study by Bennell reports that British investment in SSACs declined from 4.5% of the total overseas investment in 1978 to 0.5% in 1986. The UK being the major source of foreign investment to countries of the region it is important to find out why the decline is taking place and through the process, to indicate ways of revitalizing the flow of investment to the countries of the region by way of JVs.

Table 1.1
Population growth in SSACs and other regions of the world 1965-90
(projected to year 2000)

Country Group	1989 population (millions)	Average Annual Growth (%) 1965-73	1973-80	1980-90	1990-2000
Low- & middle-income economies	4003	2.5	2.1	2.1	1.9
Sub-Saharan Africa	479	2.6	2.8	3.2	3.1
East Asia	1566	2.7	1.7	1.5	1.4
South Asia	1132	2.4	2.4	2.3	1.9
Europe, Middle East & North Africa	404	1.9	2.1	2.1	2.1
Latin America & the Caribbean	422	2.7	2.4	2.1	1.8
High-income economies	789	1.0	0.8	0.7	0.5
Total(2)	4792	2.2	1.9	1.8	1.7

Source: Compiled from World Development Report 1990. World Bank. p. 159.

The general preference shown for the JV mode

In attempting to attract various resources from foreign sources for development, third world countries including SSACs have also shown a strong desire for local participation in ownership (Oman 1989, Cavusgil and Ghauri). In some countries where wholly-owned subsidiaries (wos) were either prohibited or discouraged JVs have been the only feasible form of investment for foreign firms. Though some recent evidences indicate that the trend in policies are towards lessening the pressure with regard to

7

the requirement of local participation, the desire for JVs is still strong in many DCs including SSACs.

Scope of the study

The food and agribusiness sector

Agribusiness is a broad subject and there is a need to segment it for a closer examination. This study focuses on the food sub-sector in its broader context to include beverage products. Thus, 'food and agribusiness' is meant to refer to primary production, manufacturing and distribution of food and drinks products.

International JVs

JVs can be formed between firms in the same country (national JVs); they can also be formed between a firm(s) in the host country on the one hand, and a firm(s) from any developed or developing country on the other (international JVs). This study focuses on international JVs, involving UK based agribusiness firms on the one hand and firms in SSACs on the other.

UK based agribusiness firms

The survey of foreign firms in this study is limited to UK based agribusiness firms for three reasons.

i)   UK based companies play significant role in DCs as sources of foreign investment in general, and in agribusiness in particular. For instance, in 1982 of the total foreign direct investment in DCs, UK share was 11%; second to the US which accounted for 48%. (Cavusgil & Ghauri). UK's share is higher than other countries of significant involvement in the international business scene: Germany (9%), Japan (8%), and France (7%). Again next to the US, UK firms predominate in investing overseas in the food industry. For instance, in 1985, of the world's 100 largest food companies 38 were US and 25 were UK based. (Oman).

ii)   Though the investment interest of UK MNCs has been shifting from DCs to the markets of the developed countries since the early 1970's

8

(Stopford 1976), the involvement of UK based firms in SSACs remained significant. For instance, Bennell's findings reveal that UK corporate investment comprises between 50 and 80% of all industrial foreign direct investment in each English-speaking African country.

iii) The third reason has to do with expediency. In addition to the above stated reasons, limiting the survey to UK based firms was found more practical in terms of administering the questionnaire, conducting face-to-face interviews, response follow-up and getting maximum results from a limited financial resources made available to the researcher.

Generalizability of findings to SSACs

The study is concerned primarily with English-speaking African countries (ESACs). However, it is believed that the findings of the research are generalizable to the SSACs because the basic characteristics are very similar. The major reasons why findings of the research apply to countries of the region are as follows:

i) ESACs account for about 55% of the total population, 66% of total value added in industrial production in SSACs, and over 90% of UK industrial investment in Africa as a whole (excluding South Africa and Namibia). (Bennell)

ii) SSACs share common economic problems: among the major ones are poor export and balance of payments records, dependence on primary products for export, low level of technological development, importance of agriculture in their economy, and the debt crisis.

iii) SSACs share the common legacy of dominant state role in their economies.

iv) SSACs share common political and economic objectives and aspirations expressed, for instance, through the Organization of African Unity, and the Lagos Plan of Action for the Economic Development of Africa. Regional economic cooperations such as the Economic Community of West African States (ECOWAS), Preferential Trade Agreement of the Eastern and Southern African States (PTA), Southern African Development Coordination

9

Conference (SADCC) are to grow and converge into the African Economic Community.

v)   SSACs share common history and social structure which have had long lasting effects on their development experiences; and which make them unique from many DCs of Asia and Latin America. For example, Killick (1992) notes that colonially-imposed national frontiers, the survival of traditional social structures, low population densities and the favorable land-labor ratio which encouraged dispersed settlements and migration had made 'personal rule and clientelist-based politics' more pervasive in countries of the region than other DCs of Asia and Latin America.

vi) More specifically, recent trends provide more evidence as to why SSACs can be considered similarly. By 1992 over 35 countries in the region were undertaking political and economic reforms giving credence to the argument that they have common political and economic problems to address. Further, an examination of the investment environment in some countries of the region, as discussed in Chapter 2, indicate similar policies towards foreign investment, JVs, privatization, priorities for economic development, incentives for investors, etc. which are basically the issues examined in this book.

Large and medium/small firms

The activities of MNCs particularly in DCs have been a subject of some controversial arguments. The role of MNCs have been described positively, as agents of change, and engines of economic development. (Hill & Paliwoda 1977, Meleka 1985, Bennell). On the other hand, MNCs have been criticized for 'short sightedness' for their concern for profits only, and not for the socio-economic development of the host country; for their dominant position discouraging the development of local industries, and sometimes for political disturbances in certain countries. (George 1977, Dinham & Hines, Najafbagy 1984).

Inspite of the arguments, the impact of MNCs in the international market place is growing, and dealing with them is a reality. Though claims of both sides of the argument can be true in various contexts, given the critical shortages of skills and technology which the MNCs have in abundance, the question for policy makers in SSACs ought to be how can they make their relations with MNCs more beneficiary to their countries without jeopardizing their respective objectives. Any involvement of MNCs in DCs is basically a form of partnership, and as evidences discussed in this study show, partnership needs understanding and compromise to succeed.

In dealing with international business relations with SSACs, however, distinguishing between large and medium/small firms of developed countries would be of importance in two respects, as discussed in a UNCTC report: a) the small transnational enterprises accounted for over half of the firms with investment abroad; and b) small and medium-size TNCs may be particularly suitable partners for the low-income countries. It is implied that SSACs may attain better success in their search for products and technologies for their development objectives from medium/small TNCs.

Therefore, identifying the possible differences in the attitudes of large and medium/small foreign firms towards JVs will have important implications for policy in countries of the region.

Organization of the book

The book is organized into 8 chapters. Chapter 1 is introduction, and outlines the research problem, major objectives, significance, and scope of the study. Chapter 2 reviews the salient characteristics of the JV phenomenon in a broader context. The discussions in this chapter include the different modes of international business involvement, definitions and classifications of JVs, the trend of joint venturing in various regions of the world, the specific role of JVs in agribusiness with particular reference to SSACs, and a framework for a working definition of a JV applicable to the study.

Chapter 3 presents a review of current literature relevant to the research problem. The emphasis is in that part of the literature concerning determinants of JV formation in DCs in general and SSACs in particular. Limitations of the literature are spelled out, and a framework that would guide the conduct of the study is developed.

The methodology of research comprising the research design, data collection, the two major research techniques applied, ie. case study and survey, and the method of data analysis are dealt with in Chapter 4. Chapter 5 presents the results of the pilot survey conducted at the early stage of the research process. The results have been instrumental in understanding the particular characteristics of the agribusiness sector, and identifying the relevant variables for the questionnaire design and the case study protocol. The major findings of the study are organized into two chapters, Chapters 6 and 7. Chapter 6 presents the results of the case study of Zimbabwe. Here, the entry environment for joint venturing in the agribusiness sector, opinions and attitudes of policy makers, executives of big and small firms, and JV partners and managers, and representatives of foreign interests are assessed and evaluated. Finally the theoretical propositions posited for this part of the research are examined and discussed. Chapter 7 is concerned with the UK part of the study. The hypotheses posited with regard to opinions and attitudes of foreign firm executives are tested using non-parametric statistical techniques.

Chapter 8 presents a summary of the research problem, methodology, and major research findings. A summary of the implications of the findings of the study for policy regarding joint venturing in the agribusiness sector in SSACs, a conclusion, and recommendations are also given in this chapter. This is followed by a discussion of the theoretical, methodological and empirical contributions, and limitations of the study. The chapter concludes with a pointer of areas for further research.

Since confidentiality of information was pledged for executives that completed the questionnaire and responded to the follow-up interviews, generally mentioning company names is avoided in the discussion of survey results. But where there was a need to illustrate by example, a code is used instead of the company name. Besides appending specific references to each chapter, the complete list of reference materials are organized into a bibliography. Research instruments used for data collection and some detail materials are given as appendices.

Notes

1.   As defined by the World Bank (World Bank 1990 p xi) sub-Saharan Africa comprises all of the countries south of the Sahara excluding South Africa, with a total population of 479 million (1989).

2.   As indicated in the 'definitions and data notes' section of the report (World Bank 1990, p.x), the total shown is that of 'reporting economies'. This total does not include the 'non-reporting economies'; namely Albania, Bulgaria, Cuba, the former Czechoslovakia, the

12

former German Democratic Republic, Democratic People's Republic of Korea, Mongolia, Namibia, and the former USSR.

References

Baum, W.C. & Tolbert, S.M. (1985). *Investing in Development: Lessons of World Bank Experience*. New York: Oxford University Press.

Beamish, P.(1987). 'Joint Ventures in LDCs: Partner Selection and Performance', *Management International Review*. Vol.27 No.1 pp.23-37.

Bennell, P.(1990). 'British Industrial Investment in Sub-Saharan Africa: Corporate Responses to Economic Crisis in the 1980s', *Development Policy Review*. vol.8 no.2 pp.155-77.

Cavusgil, S.T. & Ghauri, P.N.(1990). *Doing Business in Developing Countries: Entry and Negotiation Strategies*. London: Routledge.

Cundiff, E.W. & Hilger, M.T.(1988). *Marketing in the International Environment*. 2nd Edition. Prentice-Hall Inc.

Dinham, B. & Hines, C.(1983). *Agribusiness in Africa*. London: Earth Resources Research Ltd.

Downey, W.D. & Erickson, S.P.(1987). *Agribusiness Management*. 2nd edition. McGraw-Hill.

Economics Brief: 'The Bleak Continent', *The Economist*. December 9, 1989. pp.100-101.

Fieldman, G.M.(1987). 'US Trade Outlook: sub-Saharan Africa', *Business America*. vol.10 no.20 Sept. 28. pp.21-5.

George, S.(1977). *How the Other Half Dies: the Real Reasons for World Hunger*. Penguin Books.

Hill, R.W. & Paliwoda, S.(1977). 'Poland Favors the Multinational', *Sales Engineering*. May. pp.2-5.

Killick, T.(1992). 'Explaining Africa's Post-Independence Development Experiences', *ODI Working Paper 60*. London: ODI.

Loutfi, M.(1989). 'Development Issues and State Policies in sub-Saharan Africa', *International Labor Review*. Vol.128 no.2. pp. 137-53.

Meleka, A.H.(1985). 'The Changing Role of Multinational Corporations', *Management International Review*. vol.25 no.1. pp.36-45.

Najafbagy, R.(1984). 'Operations of Multinational Corporations and Local Enterprises in Arab Countries', *Management International Review*. vol.25 no.4. pp.46-57.

Oman, C.(1989). *New Forms of Investment in Developing Country Industries: Mining, Petrochemicals, Automobiles, Textiles, Food.* Paris: Organization for Economic Co-operation and Development (OECD).

Onah, J.O.(1989). 'The Role of Multinational Companies in the Agricultural Development of Nigeria', *Journal of International Food and Agribusiness Marketing.* Vol.1 no.2. pp.63-84.

Porter, M.(1992). 'Capital Disadvantage: America's Failing Capital Investment System', *Harvard Business Review.* vol.70 no.5. September/October. pp.65-82.

Simiar, F.(1983). 'Major Causes of JV Failures in the Middle East: the Case of Iran', *Management International Review.* pp.58-68.

Stoever, W.A.(1989). 'Why State Corporations in Developing Countries Have Failed to Attract Foreign Investment', *International Marketing Review.* vol.6 no.3. pp.62-78.

Stopford, J.M.(1976). 'Changing Perspectives on Investment by British Manufacturing Multinationals', *Journal of International Business Studies.* vol.7 no.2. pp.15-27.

Torok, S.J. et al.(1991). 'Management Assistance Needs of Small Food and Kindred Products Processors', *Agribusiness.* Vol. 7 No.5. pp.447-61.

Tuttle, R. & Buchmiller, J.(1988). 'Mauritania's Marine Fisheries Offer Untapped Commercial Opportunities for US Business', *Business America.* vol.109 no.10 May 9. pp.39-40.

UNCTC (1988). *Transnational Corporations in World Development: Trends & Prospects.* New York: United Nations.

UNIDO (1989). *Agro-processing Overview. Program Development Support Unit (PDSU).* Winter Report, December. (unpublished monograph).

World Bank (1990). *World Development Report 1990.* New York: Oxford University Press.

_____ (1988). *World Development Report 1988.* New York: Oxford University Press.

2 The JV phenomenon: An overview

Introduction

Joint ventures (JVs) are often confused with other modes of business participation, particularly with licensing, countertrade and contract manufacturing. The term 'joint venture' is also employed in a wide variety of ways, from tentative arrangement between two or more interested parties for achieving a short term goal to establishing on-going ventures involving huge resources. For the purpose of clarity, therefore, a framework for tackling the particular research problem needs be provided.

First, the salient characteristics of the main international business involvement modes are discussed. Next, the various definitions and applications of the JV concept, and their classifications are reviewed. The popularity of JVs has been growing not only in developing countries (DCs) but also in the developed economies. The evidences that show this trend are reviewed briefly. The section that follows outlines the role JVs can play and the role they have played so far in the agribusiness sector in sub-Saharan African countries (SSACs). This section is augmented by a description of some cases of joint agribusiness venture experiences from some SSACs. Finally, drawing from the preceding discussions a working definition of a JV as applied in this study is developed.

Forms of international business involvement

The different forms of international business involvement of firms, of which JVs are a part have been described by many authors including Auster

(1987), Oman (1989), Paliwoda, Fraser and Hite (1988), and Cavusgil and Ghauri (1990). While Oman dealt with mainly the investment types of business involvement, discussions of Paliwoda, and Cavusgil and Ghauri were broader and include various trading involvements of firms.

Oman distinguishes between two forms of foreign investment: traditional foreign direct investment (FDI), and new forms of investment (NFI). FDI has been the main form of foreign investment upto the mid 1970's, after which its role was gradually taken up by NFI. NFI includes JVs, licensing agreements, turnkey contracts, production sharing and risk-service contracts, and international subcontracting. Some operations combine two or more of these arrangements. In NFI, generally the foreign company provides goods towards the project while the host country keeps the majority or whole ownership of the project.

Different terms have been applied to describe what Oman called NFI. For example, Auster terms such arrangements as 'international corporate linkages'. Harrigan (1987), and Forest (1990) use the term 'strategic alliance', and Morris and Hergert (1987) term them as 'international collaborative agreements'. Fraser & Hite discuss 'compensation': where a company sells a plant, equipment, or technology to another company or government in exchange for an output from those goods. They propose that this form may be an alternative for DCs to get advanced technology without hard cash. However, this description is very similar to Paliwoda's 'industrial cooperation agreements', and Cavusgil and Ghauri's 'contract manufacturing' and is not therefore treated as an additional and a new form of business involvement.

The major forms of international business involvement by firms as described by Cavusgil and Ghauri include: a) indirect exporting, b) direct exporting, c) licensing, d) contract manufacturing, e) management contracts, f) foreign production and marketing /direct investment/ (this may take broadly two forms: wos and JVs), and g) countertrade.

Defining JVs

A JV has been broadly defined as an entity formed between two or more partners for their mutual benefit (Friedmann & Kalmanoff 1961, Tomlinson 1970, Cundiff & Hilger 1988, Herzfeld 1989, Harrigan 1986). Friedmann and Kalmanoff's definition of a JV as "..any form of association which implies collaboration for more than a very transitory period" is widely applied. But as the authors themselves indicated the definition is too broad, and therefore, cannot serve as a working definition. For instance, the definition does not indicate on the purpose and form of such collaboration. Subsequent definitions attempted to be more precise. Tomlinson, for example, defines a JV as: "the commitment, for more than a very short duration, of funds, facilities, and services by two or more legally separate interests, to an enterprise for their mutual benefit". (p.8)

While these definitions highlight the basic characteristics of a JV, there are variations due to the emphasis placed on the detail of the partnership or cooperation. In the following paragraphs some of the variations in the definition and application of the JV phenomenon are discussed.

Nature of the business

Some definitions emphasize the nature of the business activity undertaken by the JV partnership. This can be illustrated by two definitions given by Cundiff & Hilger, and Paliwoda (1981). Cundiff and Hilger, give a definition of a JV as "..the method for entering foreign markets whereby a firm shares ownership in the foreign investment with local partners" (p.576). Here, the international nature of the relationship, share in ownership, and JV as a market entry strategy are emphasized. On the other hand, Paliwoda in his study of JVs in East European countries gives the definition as "..joint-equity ventures between Western companies and East European enterprises, located within East Europe" (p.viii). This definition specifies the regional origin of the partners and the equity basis of the cooperation.

Organizational aspect of the venture

In some definitions of a JV, formation of a separate enterprise is emphasized (Tomlinson, Pfeffer & Selancik 1978, Harrigan 1988). Pfeffer & Selancik, for example, describe a JV as "..a new, separate, organizational entity..". Harrigan defines JVs as "business agreements whereby two or more owners create a *separate entity*" (emphasis Harrigan). However, this is not always the case in what are known as 'contractual JVs' (or industrial cooperation).

Partners

Generally, JVs are understood to be inter-firm relations, be they private, public or state-owned. Some authors extend the application of the JV

17

concept to inter-regional cooperations. An example is a study by Svetlicic (1986) entitled 'investment promotion measures: experience of regional regimes for JVs'. Svetlicic reports about a number of JV schemes: 6 in Latin America, 4 in Asia and 3 in Africa. Among these JV schemes are Multinational Industrial Enterprises, East African Industries, and Mano River Union Industries (in Africa); Andean Multinational Enterprises, Caricom Enterprises, and Central American Integration Industries (in Latin America); and Asean Industrial JVs (in Asia). As Svetlicic explains, these are regional country groupings to promote investment and trade among them. This departs from the conventional meaning of a JV, which is a form of partnership between firms.

Foreign participation

In some cases, particularly in reference to DCs, any foreign participation short of wos is considered as a JV relationship. For instance, Najafbagy (1985), in his study of operations of MNCs and local enterprises in Arab countries discusses six types of 'JVs' operating in Kuwait: (shareholding companies, closed joint stock companies, limited companies, joint liability companies, limited partnership companies, and private investors). Though he did not give any concept or definition of a JV, it appears from his discussion that one criterion for some of the types mentioned is any form of foreign participation in Kuwait.

Duration of partnership

Though most definitions mention the partnership to last for some reasonable period of time, for 'more than a very short duration' as the definition given by Tomlinson and cited above stipulates, there is no indication as to what the acceptable duration span is. A case of interest in this aspect is the 'JV' program administered by the Department of Trade and Industry (DTI), UK. In this arrangement, the DTI assists British firms to participate in various shows, conferences, and missions at concessionary costs (AEA, 1990). This type of cooperation between the DTI and a particular firm is a one-off undertaking, lasting the duration of the event, which in any case is a matter of months, or shorter. In its application, the JV concept appears to be used inspite of the short duration of the cooperation.

Management control

Another element, ignored by the various definitions, but nevertheless is an important characteristic of JVs is the role of management control. While the pooling of resources is emphasized, the need in the share of management decision making is seldom mentioned. This element is a point of departure from other forms of partnerships, generally termed as passive financial relations (Harrigan), agencies (Najafbagy), portfolio-like investments (Beamish 1988).

Level of resource contribution

It is generally pointed out that resource contribution is the major basis for JV formation. However, there is no general agreed level of resources as the minimum or the maximum to be contributed by the respective partners. This partly accounts for the confusion between JVs and other partnerships or financial investments. Herzfeld (1989) is of the opinion that the share of ownership between partners is of secondary importance as long as the JV is controlled by all partners, none dominating the other(s). Beamish (1988) in his study of JVs in DCs defined JVs as "..shared-equity undertakings between two or more parties, each of which holds at least 5% of the equity". (p.3).

However, some indicate that the level of 5% is too low for any partner to make any significant impact with the affairs of the JV. For instance, Choudhury (1989) in his study of determinants of successes and failures in international JV suggested 25% as the minimum share of a partner in a JV. Herzfeld also cites the works of Young and Bradford who suggested that shares should not go outside a 60% to 40% range.

Classifying JVs

Classification based on equity

Two broad basis of classifying JVs are generally used. The first is, whether a JV partnership is based on equity. Thus, a JV is either 'equity JV' or a 'non-equity JV', the later alternately termed as 'industrial cooperation' or 'contractual agreements'. Paliwoda (1986) discusses the two types of JVs as: a) 'joint-equity ventures', where "..each of the respective partners contributes a sum either in equity or technological know-how towards capital participation, and with no fixed duration..", and b) 'contractual JVs/industrial cooperation', where "..economic relationship and activities arise from contracts ...providing for reciprocal transfer of one or more commercial assets...to meet specific objectives of the contracting parties". (p.90). Such industrial cooperations are expressed in various forms: a) payment in kind for delivery of plant and equipment, b) co-production, c)specialization, d) joint marketing e) project cooperation, f) contract manufacturing & subcontracting, and g) joint research and development (Paliwoda 1975).

Within the joint equity ventures, further types are identified as: majority JV (more than 50%), coownership (50-50%), and minority JV (less than 50%), in proportion to the contributions of the particular partner of interest to equity capital of the enterprise. For instance, in international JVs where a foreign partner is involved, the JV can be a (foreign) majority JV, a (foreign) minority JV, or a coownership, depending on the share of the foreign partner. Generally, majority ownership is sought by the respective partners as this would imply managerial control of the venture.

Classification based on nationality and location

The second basis of classifying JVs is on nationality of the partners, and the operational location of the JV. On these criteria, Tomlinson identifies four types of JVs:

National JVs: formed between two or more interests from the same country;

Foreign international JVs: formed by partners of different nationalities in a third host country without including any partner from the host country;

International JVs: formed between host nationals (but excluding any government participation) and foreign firm(s), and;

Mixed international JVs or (mixed ventures): where the host government is involved as a partner with foreign firms.

Other basis of classifications

Further classification are possible depending on the purpose for such a classification. For example, Goldenberg (1989) identifies four forms of JVs based on the operational aspect of the ventures: manufacturing JVs, marketing JVs, processing JVs, and joint research and development. Habib and Burnett (1989) discuss a classification based on 'functional activities': manufacturing, sales and services, extraction and other. Using the same basis, Linklaters & Paines and Nightingale (1990) cite from an OECD report which came up with a longer list of JV types: a) research and development, b) natural resources exploration and exploitation, c) engineering and construction, d) production/manufacturing e) buying and selling, and f) services.

The trend in JV formation

The literature highlights the rationale for JV formation as the fulfillment of the needs and objectives of the parties involved, which otherwise would have been difficult or impossible to achieve with other business participation alternatives. In the case of host countries the attraction stems from the conviction that JVs enable them to acquire technology, capital, and skills with participation in ownership, control and profits. For the foreign firms adopting this strategy facilitates easy entry to markets and access to resources, and also minimizes risks (Auster, Beamish 1988, Goldenberg, Harrigan 1986, Oman, Wright and Russell 1975).

It is further noted, therefore, that joint venturing has become a popular type of investment pursued by both foreign firms and host countries. For instance, the number of JVs in East European countries including the former USSR grew from 43 in 1980 to 680 in 1984, and to 831 by 1987 (UN 1989). In the Peoples Republic of China JVs grew from a mere 200 in 1983 to a total of more than 3,200 by 1986 (Shenkar 1990).

JVs are growing as the major strategy for firms in the economically advanced (Western) countries both for expansion within the developed countries and to DCs. Key et al. (1987) point out that between 1982 and 1985 531 JVs were registered in the 'market economy industrialized countries'. Harrigan (1988) notes that though JVs have existed 'since antiquity', they have mushroomed since the mid 1970's in the US. By 1983 the number of JVs was so large that they accounted for almost one-third of all firms active in some industries. Harrigan predicts that more JVs "..will undoubtedly be launched in the wake of increasingly rapid rates of technological changes, deregulation and globalization". (p.143).

Eales (1990) reports that in Europe collaboration has become the fashion: in the wake of 1992, companies are going more and more into JVs.

21

In the last 3 months of 1989 alone 669 deals, ranging from 'full-blown JVs to tiny high-tech research links' were set up. Though it is indicative of the rise of JV as an important business organization mode, two shortcomings have to be noticed about the data provided by Eales. The data covers a very short period of time, and the data does not distinguish between JVs and other types of partnerships. Fig. 2.1 shows the number of firms that establishing JVs and other partnerships by business sector.

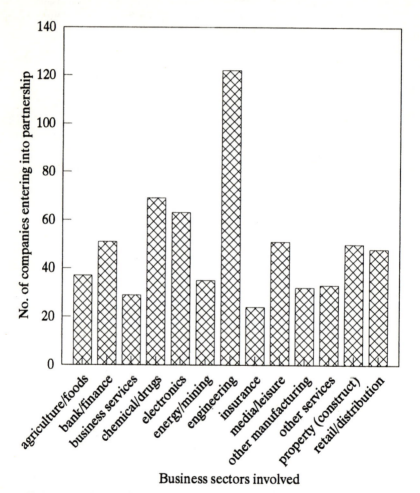

Business sectors involved

Source: Eales, 1990. p.28.

Fig 2.1 Number of West European companies entering into partnership by business sector (October - December 1989)

Most firms forming such cooperation arrangements appear to be engineering firms. Firms engaged in the manufacture of chemicals/drugs, and electronics, and in services such as banking, and leisure appear to be more inclined to form partnerships. Fig. 2.2 shows the number of firms setting up partnerships by country in Europe. According to these data, German firms are the keenest to enter into partnerships followed by British and French firms.

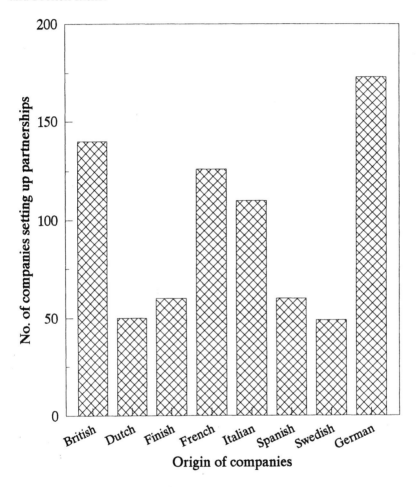

Source: Eales, 1990. p.28

Fig.2.2 Number of West European companies setting up partnerships by company origin (October - December 1989)

Most of the partnerships formed by the firms indicated above are within Western Europe (53% of the 669), followed by Eastern Europe (36%), and the rest of the world accounting for only 11%.

Hill (1981) notes that about half of the subsidiaries of US and UK firms in DCs are run as JVs. The proportions for Japanese and continental European firms are much higher: the Japanese firms have local partners in 90% of their foreign subsidiaries, while the percentage for continental Europe is 60%.

Though figures are scarce with regard to SSACs, those available provide important clues. Friedmann and Kalmanoff show that since the 1950's JVs have been formed in Kenya, Nigeria and Ghana between UK firms and African local interests, in many cases the government of the concerned country. The JVs were mainly in mining (extractive) and agriculture (plantations) sectors. The major UK company mentioned as partner in the JVs was Unilever, through its holding companies: East Africa Industries Ltd, and United Africa Company Ltd. Some recent JVs in the agribusiness sector in SSACs are discussed in Appendix A.

Afriyie (1988) points out that in the period between 1980 and 1984, JVs accounted for about 40% of all manufacturing firms employing 30 or more persons in Ghana. The corresponding percentages for foreign wos and local firms were 4% and 56% of the manufacturing firms respectively. He further noted that there has been a dramatic shift in ownership since the 1960's in Ghana, from foreign wholly owned to JVs. In Nigeria 427 business permits for JVs involving foreign firms have been approved in mid 1992 (West Africa 1992).

Further, there is evidence to suggest that many of the other SSACs have taken various steps to promote JVs. Table 2.1 shows the changes in investment laws designed to encourage JVs and the years they came to effect for some African countries. Table 2.2 and table 2.3 summarize the foreign investment environment in some Eastern and southern African countries compiled from various sources. The tables outline the policy on JVs, the incentives provided, the areas of policy emphasis, the trend in privatization and other related factors. Overall, the indications are that SSACs have reviewed their investment policies recently in a manner to encourage foreign investment in general and JVs in particular.

There has also been a growing trend towards privatization in many SSACs as indicated in the tables. Parastatals have been generally considered inefficient, draining public money; and privatizing them is considered as a way to bring better efficiency and saving/increasing government revenues. Some countries have gone some way in the actual privatization of parastatals (e.g. Niger, Guinea, Togo and Senegal), and some have completed the preparation stage for privatizing most state-owned firms (e.g. Nigeria, Kenya, Uganda) (UNCTC 1988, UNIDO 1989b).

Table 2.1
Changes in investment laws in some SSACs

Country name	Investment law	Year implemented
Ethiopia	Investment Code 1989	1989
Ghana	Investment Code (PNDC Law 116)	1985
Kenya	Foreign Investment Protection Act	1989
Mozambique	Law 4/84	1984
Nigeria	Enterprises Decree'89 & Companies Decree'90	1990
Sudan	Encouragement of Investment Act	1980
Tanzania	National Investment Promotion Policy	1982
Uganda	Investment Code 1991	1991
Zambia	Foreign Investment Act 1986	1986
Zimbabwe	Investment Promotion policy & Regulation	1989

Source: Compiled from various UNIDO, UNCTC publications, country reports and newspapers.

Table 2.2 The investment environment in some Eastern African countries

	Ethiopia	Kenya	Tanzania	Uganda
Applicable laws	Investment code 1989	Foreign Investment Protection Act	National Investment Promotion Policy	Investment Code 1991
Policy on JVs	Only mode for foreign investment	generally no restriction; some support	strongly encouraged	generally no restrictions; some support
Limitations on foreign ownership	49% upper limit	no upper limit	no upper limit	no upper limit
Dominant enterprises	parastatals	mixed; parastatals & private	parastatals	parastatals
Privatization policy	recent change to encourage private sector	privatizing parastatals underway	recent change to encourage private sector	privatizing parastatals underway
Incentives - Tariff protection	available; various	available; various	-----	-----

Table 2.2 cont'd

	Ethiopia	Kenya	Tanzania	Uganda
Tax rates	5 years tax holiday; 40% corp. tax	2-5 years tax holiday	up to 5 years holiday; 50% corp. tax	up to 5 years tax holiday
Duty & customs	exemption on capital goods; exports & some imports	exemptions vary 50-100%	exemptions vary & conditional	exemptions on capital goods
Access to domestic credit	-----	20-60% of capital	-----	-----
Profit repatriation	no restrictions	no restrictions	up to 50% of 'retention scheme'	no restrictions
Other incentives	income tax exemption for foreign staff	input price control; investment allowance	income tax exemption for proprietors	-----
Infrastructure	limited to urban areas	well developed	limited; need upgrading	landlocked; basically fair; need rehabilitation

Table 2.2 cont'd

	Ethiopia	Kenya	Tanzania	Uganda
One-stop approval systems	----	the IPC	the IPC	Uganda Investment Authority
Free trade zones	----	Inbond mfging schemes	designated special growth centres	----
Protection from nationalization	guaranteed by law	guaranteed by law (nationalization prohibited)	guaranteed by law	----
Dispute settlement arrangement	to be dealt with in contract agreement	member of MIGA & ICISD	member of MIGA & ICISD	----
Investment priorities & objectives	agriculture; mfging; technology; forex; employment	employment; rural devt; forex; technology	agriculture; technology; forex; decentralization	agriprocessing; forex; rehabilitation of industry; employment

Table 2.2 cont'd

(Note: ----- means data not available)

Sources: Ethiopian Trade Journal, 7 (2/3) 1989
IPC: Kenya, 1988
Newsweek, April 1991
Planning Commission, Tanzania (undated)
UNIDO (1989b)

Abbreviations:
Forex: foreign exchange
FTZ: free trade zone
ICC: International Chamber of Commerce
ICISD: International Centre for the
          Settlement of Investment Disputes
IPC: Investment Promotion Centre
MIGA: Mulitnational Investment Guarantee Agency

29

Table 2.3 The investment environment in some Southern African countries

	Malawi	Mozambique	Zambia	Zimbabwe
Applicable laws	-----	Law 4/84 of 1984	Foreign Investment Act 1986	Investment Promotion Policy & Regulation 1989
Policy on JVs	strongly encouraged	strongly encouraged	-----	encouraged
Limitations on foreign ownership	no upper limit	-----	no upper limit	no upper limit
Dominant enterprises	mixed; states role increasing	parastatals	mixed; parastatals & private	mixed; parastatals & private
Privatization policy	-----	recent change to encourage private sector	-----	-----
Incentives - Tarrif protection	-----	-----	-----	selective

Table 2.3 cont'd

	Malawi	Mozambique	Zambia	Zimbabwe
Tax rates	50% reduction for first 5 years	2-10 years tax holiday	10 years tax holiday	corp income tax 52%; with various allowances
Duty & customs	exemption nominal on capital goods	-----	exemption on inputs for export	-----
Access to domestic credit	some restrictions	-----	preferential access for agriculturists	-----
Profit repatriation	no restrictions	'exportable profits' allowed	net of tax	depends on balance of payment situation
Other incentives	-----	tax free import for foreign staff	access to land; various for exporters	investment allowance; various for exporters
Infrastructure	landlocked; high transport costs	needs rehabilitation	landlocked; fairly developed links	landlocked; well developed links

Table 2.3 cont'd

	Malawi	Mozambique	Zambia	Zimbabwe
One-stop approval systems	-----	-----	the IPC	the ZIC
Free trade zones	-----	special conditions in FTZs	FTZ (planned)	-----
Protection from nationalization	-----	guaranteed by law	guaranteed by law	-----
Dispute settlement arrangement	-----	dispute settled at ICC	member of MIGA & ICISD	-----
Investment priorities & objectives	value added; import substitution; employment; forex	rehabilitation of industries; agriculture; forex; technology	agribased; forex; employment; technology	processing; rural development; employment; forex; technology

Table 2.3 cont'd

(Note: ----- means data not available)

Sources: Investment Act,.1990, Zambia
UNIDO (1989b)

Abbreviations:
Forex: foreign exchange
FTZ: free trade zone
ICC: International Chamber of Commerce
ICISD: International Centre for the Settlement of
Investment Disputes
IPC: Investment Promotion Centre
MIGA: Multinational Investment Guarantee Agency
ZIC: Zimbabwe Investment Centre

33

JVs and agribusiness

Agribusiness encompasses the complex organizational and operational systems that provide the various inputs to the farming sector, and enterprises that market, process and distribute agricultural and food products. Therefore, as agribusiness is a vast and complex sector, there is a need to identify a specific sub-sector for study. Thus, the focus here will be on the determinants for JVs in the agro-production, processing and marketing sub-sector.

The importance of agro-industries in the economic development of DCs and the various constraints they have encountered are highlighted in Abbott (1988), Srivastava (1989), Parkinson (1985), and UNIDO (1989). Agro-industries are credited with: a) stimulating domestic markets, b) product development through processing, branding, and packaging to meet international as well as domestic market specifications, c) enhancing sustainable development through backward and forward linkages, d) providing growing income to the farmer (through market expansion with processed products and value addition), and e) more balanced distribution of industries as agro-industries are generally located around raw material sources. Agricultural produces can go through various processes each time fetching additional value. Depending on the type of the raw material processed, the added value can be several folds of the initial value. In the examples discussed by Srivastava from experiences in India, the added values range from about 70% in the case of processing shrimps, to about 500% in the case of leather products.

The agro-processing and marketing sector in SSACs is characterized by inadequacies in raw materials quality and supplies, appropriate technology, marketing infrastructure and, financial resources (including foreign currencies). Moreover, in advancing from primary processing to secondary processing the capital investment, technological complexity and managerial requirements also increase, compounding the problems mentioned above. Governments of many African countries, as those in other DCs, have attempted to overcome the problems of foreign exchange, technology and skills through inviting foreign companies from economically advanced countries.

Evidences discussed in the preceding sections indicate that SSACs have favored JVs as a means of acquiring resources in short supply for their development. And where JVs have been successfully formed, as can be seen from some cases outlined in Appendix A, the benefits are quite impressive. Besides the acquisition of capital, creation of employment, human resource development through training, and revenues from taxation and exports; a general stimulation of economic and service activities have been attained. However, setting up successful JVs is acknowledged to be a difficult task. For instance, it is noted that out of some 50 agricultural JVs set up in Nigeria in the mid 1980's, only about 10 were said to be viable by 1990 (BNC 1990).

A framework for a working definition of a JV

As shown in the preceding sections of the chapter, the JV concept is broad, and there is a need to set boundaries to be able to focus in the area of interest. JVs in this study will have the following characteristics.

i)   The study is concerned with determinants of JV formation in one sector: the food and agribusiness sector. The food and agribusiness sector is defined to consist of farm production, processing (manufacturing), distribution and marketing of food and drinks products.

ii)   Based on nationality of partners and location of the venture, JVs were classified into four types: national, foreign international, international, and mixed international. As the study focuses on JVs involving UK firms on the one hand, and firms in SSACs on the other, the relevant types are international and mixed international. However, the basis of the distinction between the two, i.e., the involvement of government as host partner in the JV, is not of primary interest for the research. Therefore, a JV refers to a venture formed by a partnership of a foreign partner(s) on the one hand, and a host partner(s) who are nationals of the host country on the other.

iii)   Partners of interest for the study are: a) the foreign partner(s) are UK based food and agribusiness firms. Such firms may be private, public or quasi-government organizations, and b) the host partner(s) are any private, state-owned, public owned firms in the agribusiness sectors of SSACs.

iv)   Where the commitment of equity capital by either party, the foreign partner(s) or the host partner(s), is not less than 25% of the total, the venture is considered as equity based JV.

v) Where the resource contribution of one of the parties (most often the foreign partner) is limited to one or a combination of management, technical, marketing infrastructure, etc. the venture is considered a non-equity JV. As discussed previously in this chapter, African economies suffer from the lack or shortage of these resources, and therefore, the participation of foreign firms based on these resources merit equal attention to those of equity based participations. Besides, as pointed out by Freidmann and Kalmanoff, such cooperations constitute a prelude to a more permanent association involving a later investment of equity capital in the venture by the foreign partner.

vi) A JV should also be differentiated from other types of agreements, such as sales/purchase agreements and projects. In addition to the conditions set above, where the agreement specifies that the venture is a going concern, and operates on profit making basis, it is considered as a JV.

The working definition of a JV for the study is:

a business venture in the food and agribusiness sector established in an African country by a partnership of a foreign firm(s) with an African private, public or state owned firm(s) based on an agreement on the respective contributions of resources, share of management control, profit and risks.

Summary and conclusions

The JV concept is defined and applied in various ways to meet the specific objectives of the studies. Among the variations are the purpose, the duration, the nature of organization of the JV. Classifications are similarly varied to fit particular purposes and interests, and they are often based on nationality of partners, whether the JV is based on equity, and on the nature of the operation of the JV.

While the need for, and exchange of resources is the basis of all JVs, specific motives may vary according to the origin of the specific firms. JVs between western industrialized country firms are the outcome of corporate strategies to meet the specific objective of the respective parent firms. Such

JVs are often formed between 'equal partners' and in areas of advanced technology. For instance, Key et al. pointed out that of the JVs formed between 1982 and 1985 in the 'market economy industrialized countries', about 73% were in the 'science based sectors'. On the other hand, JVs formed in DCs tend to seek various resources to improve or modernize basic production operations. Thus, in many DCs JVs are sought for with the wider intentions of acquiring capital, technology, and financial resources; and skills involving managerial, technical, marketing and financial. The host partner usually is in a weaker position in terms of the uniqueness of the resources and attributes he is to contribute towards the JV. Socialist countries seek for partners to modernize and specialize their industries through acquisition of advanced technology, and also to some extent technical and managerial know-how.

Due to the peculiar characteristics of JVs in exchange of resources and attributes, they are growing in popularity in both the developed countries and DCs. SSACs have increasingly attempted to promote JVs, and a review of some JVs in the agribusiness sector of SSACs shows that they resulted in significant benefits to partners and host countries concerned. To set the boundaries and context of the study a working definition of a JV is proposed. Given that successful JVs are useful and desirable in SSACs, the next question to tackle is what determines their formation in the agribusiness sector of SSACs? In order to tackle this question, first the literature on the motives for joint venturing, and the determinants of JV formation are reviewed in the next chapter.

References

Abbott, J.C.(1988). *Agricultural Processing for Development*. Aldershot: Gower Publishing Co. Ltd.

AEA (the Agricultural Engineers Association), *Overseas Information Bulletin*, Week 37, 14 Sept., 1990.

Auster, E.R.(1987). 'International Corporate Linkages: Dynamic Forms in changing Environments', *The Columbia Journal of World Business*. vol.22 no.2. pp.3-6.

Beamish, P.W.(1988). *Multinational Joint Ventures in Developing Countries*. London: Routledge.

BNC (British-Nigeria Chamber of Commerce). A note presented at a seminar on 'Export Opportunities in the Agriculture Sectors in Nigeria and Kenya'. 29 November 1990. Department of Trade and Industry. London.

Cavusgil, S.T.& Ghauri, P.N.(1990). *Doing Business in Developing Countries: Entry and Negotiation Strategies.* Routledge: London.

Choudhury, M.A.J.(1989). International Joint Ventures: Some Interfirm-Organization Specific Determinants of Successes and Failures: a Factor Analytic Exploration. unpublished PhD Thesis. Temple University.

Council of State Special Decree No.11/1989. (1989). *The Ethiopian Trade Journal.* vol.8 no.2-3. pp.35-42.

Cundiff, E.W. & Hilger, M.T.(1988). *Marketing in the International Environment.* 2nd Edition. Prentice Hall.

Downey, W.D. & Erickson, S.P.(1987). *Agribusiness Management.* 2nd Edition. McGraw-Hill.

Forrest, J.E.(1990). 'Strategic Alliances and Small Technology-Based Firm', *Journal of Small Business Management.* vol.28 no.3. pp.37-45.

Fraser, C. & Hite, R.E.(1988). 'Compensation as an Alternative to Ownership in Developing Markets: Beliefs, Attitudes and Uses', *Journal of World Trade.* vol.22 no.6. December. pp.95-106.

Friedmann, W.G. & Kalmanoff, G.(1961). *Joint International Business Ventures.* New York: Columbia University Press.

George, S.(1977). *How the Other Half Dies: the Real Reasons for World Hunger.* Penguin Books.

Goldenberg, S.(1989). *International Joint Ventures in Action.* Hutchinson Business Books.

Government of Zambia (1990). The Investment Act, 1990. Lusaka. (draft monograph).

Habib, G.M. & Burnett, J.J.(1989). 'An Assessment of Channel Behavior in an Alternative Structural Arrangement: the International Joint Venture', *International Marketing Review.* vol.6 no.3. pp.7-21.

Harrigan, K.R.(1988). 'Joint Ventures and Competitive Strategy', *Strategic Management Journal.* Vol.9 no.2. pp.141-58.

_____ (1987). 'Strategic Alliances: Their New Role in Global Competition', *The Columbia Journal of World Business.* vol.22 no.2. pp.67-9.

_____ (1986). *Managing for Joint Venture Success.* Lexington: Heath & Co.

Herzfeld, E.(1989). *Joint Ventures.* 2nd edition. Jordans.

Hill, R.(1981). 'Are Multinationals Aliens in the Third World?', *International Management.* January. pp.12-6.

38

IPC (Investment Promotion Centre) (1989). Investors' Guide to Kenya: Volume II. Nairobi.

Kay, N. et al. (1987). 'An Approach to the Analysis of Joint Ventures', *Working Paper No.87/313*. Florence: European University Institute (EUI).

Kristensen, E.(1987). 'Proof that a Joint Venture Can Work', *The Courier* (March-April) No.102. pp.98-9.

Linklaters & Paines and Nightingale, C.(1990). *Joint Ventures*. 1st edition. London: Longman Group UK Ltd.

Morris, D. & Hergert, M.(1987). 'Trends in International Collaborative Agreements', *The Columbia Journal of World Business*. vol.22 no.2 pp.15-21.

Najafbagy, R.(1985). 'Operations of MNCs and Local Enterprise in Arab Countries', *Management International Review*. vol.25 no.4. pp.46-57.

'Nigerian Companies in Joint Ventures' (1992). *West Africa*. May 11-17. p.804.

Oman, C.(1989). *New Forms of Investment in Developing Country Industries*. Paris: OECD.

Paliwoda, S.J.(1986). *International Marketing*. London: Heinemann Professional Publishers.

_____, (1981). *Joint East West Marketing and Production Ventures*. Gower Publishing Co. Ltd

_____, (1975). Changing Trends in Polish Trade. unpublished MSc Dissertation. Bradford University.

Parkinson, J.M.(1985). 'Marketing in Lesser Developed Countries', *The Quarterly Review of Marketing*. vol.11 no.1. Autumn. pp.12-5.

Pfeffer, J. & Salancik, G.R.(1978). *The External Control of Organizations*. New York: Harper & Row.

Planning Commission (1990, February). National Investment Promotion Policy, Tanzania. Dar Es Salaam. (draft monograph).

Shenkar, O.(1990). 'International Joint Ventures' Problems in China: Risks & Remedies', *Long Range Planning*. vol.23 no.3. pp.82-90.

Srivastava, U.K.(1989). 'Agro-processing Industries: Potential, Constraints, and Tasks Ahead', *Indian Journal of Agricultural Economics*. July-September. vol.6 no.3. pp.242-55.

Svetlicic, M. (1986). 'Investment Promotion Measures: Experience of Regional Regimes for Joint Ventures', Paper delivered at the Symposium on Selective preferential arrangements between developed and developing countries. November 28-30. Helsinki.

Tomlinson, J.W.C.(1970). *The Joint Venture Process in International Business: India & Pakistan.* Cambridge: MIT Press.

'Uganda Welcomes Investors' (1991). *Newsweek.* April 29. (Special Advertizement Section).

UN (1989). *Joint Ventures as a Form of International Economic Cooperation.* New York: Taylor & Francis.

UNCTC (1988). *Transnational Corporation in World Development: Trends and Prospects.* New York: United Nations.

UNIDO (1989a). Agro-processing Overview, Winter Report, December 12. (unpublished).

UNIDO (1989b). PTA: Investor's Guide. (monograph).

Wright, R.W. & Russel, C.S.(1975). 'Joint Ventures in Developing Countries: Realities and Responses', *The Columbia Journal of World Business.* (summer). pp.74-80.

3 Literature review: Motives for and determinants of JV formation

Introduction

This chapter reviews the joint venture (JV) literature relevant to the research problem., i.e. how determinants of foreign firm entry into JVs in developing countries (DCs) have been covered. The chapter has 3 major sections. In the first section of the chapter the literature with regard to the motives of partners for joint venturing are discussed. Literature on why firms and governments of DCs are attracted to joint venturing are reviewed. Some arguments against JVs are also discussed in this section.

The second section deals with the major determinants of JV formation in DCs. The three major determinants identified: country specific, industry specific and firm specific factors are discussed in detail, in the context of JV formation in the agribusiness sector of DCs, including sub-Saharan African countries (SSACs). The last section of the chapter presents some comments on the literature which has been reviewed. Besides identifying the major limitations of the literature, Gullander's entry determinants model is adjusted in light of additional information from the literature to tackle the specific research problem at hand: examining determinants of JV formation in the agribusiness sector of SSACs.

Motives for entry into JVs

Why firms resort to JVs

The reasons for entering into JVs is an issue widely discussed in the literature. Studies of Friedmann and Kalmanoff (1961), Gullander (1976a, 1976b), Killing (1983), Harrigan (1985), Artisien (1985), Auster (1987), Harrison (1987), Davidson (1982), Beamish (1988), Habib and Burnett (1989), Goldenberg (1989), Kent (1991) show that JVs are part of the corporate strategy of firms to achieve their corporate objectives; and are based on an exchange of resources between the independent firms involved. Through JVs firms share resources and risks, expand in the existing markets or to new markets, diversify or divest. Habib and Burnett use the term 'symbiotic marketing', first coined by Adler in 1966 to refer to cooperation between firms in a JV. Symbiotic marketing is defined as "..an alliance of resources or program between 2 or more independent organizations designed to increase the market potential of each". (P.7).

Gullander (1976a) summarizes the major reasons for entry into JVs as: a) to satisfy nationalistic demands, b) to benefit from economies of scale, critical mass and the experience curve effect, c) to decrease dependency on other firms, and d) to circumvent market imperfections. Goldenberg points out that, today even the biggest companies lack the money, time and talent for sole efforts. Therefore each firm benefits from the others strength from sharing costs, technical and marketing expertise, gaining market share, and production efficiency. Auster stresses that joint research and development allows synergy in pursuing innovation. Other reasons why firms resort to joint venturing include: as a strategy to avoid mergers and takeovers, to leap-frog protectionist barriers, JVs provide the freedom for continued rivalry as well as multiple associations, JVs permit greater control than appointing local agents, distributors, or licensing, and JVs also shorten leadtime. (Harrison, Harrigan 1988, Gullander 1976a).

While the motives discussed above are applicable to JVs in general, in international JVs the quest for expanded markets; sales of technology & components and access to natural resources consist the main motivations. (Dawson 1987, Block 1987, Connoly 1984). Given conducive situations exist in the host country, the market expansion opportunity appears to weigh heavily among the motivations of the home firm. Block pointed out that the foreign investor is more inclined to go partner when this offers access to local and regional markets. The major motives of the host partner can be identified as follows from the works of Oman 1989, Artisien, and

Beamish: acquiring modern technology; foreign exchange (access to foreign markets); acquiring capital (in the form of machinery, equipment, cash in foreign exchange); acquiring managerial, technical, marketing and financial skills; business strategy (planning); training of personnel; and use of the reputation of an established multinational company (brand name).

Host companies from countries with considerable industrial and infrastructral base had relatively little difficulty in attracting foreign investors. For instance, the success of some countries in Asia and Latin America (e.g. China, Thailand, Indonesia and Chile) in attracting foreign investors is attributed to market size, relatively high saving ratios, quality of infrastructure, the level of industrialization, and existing stock of foreign investment (Chen 1990, Dodwell 1992), which generally are lacking in most African countries. In such cases, both partners would benefit from the complementarity of their respective technologies, higher potential for joint research and development, and efficiency in production systems. This accounted partly for the growing interest by foreign and host parties for joint venturing in such countries as China, the former USSR, India, Brazil, the former Yugoslavia, etc.

Why host governments of DCs favor JVs

The reasons why governments of DCs prefer JVs to other forms of foreign participation are studied by Wright & Russell (1975), Stoever (1989), Beamish (1985), Shenkar (1990), Raveed and Renforth (1983), Oman. The literature highlights that the basic reason for preferring JVs by governments of DCs is that JVs are understood as a strategy of compromising the strong fear of domination by foreign interests on the one hand, and the strong desire for self-reliance, and control of the economy by governments of DCs on the other. Particularly during the periods until the 1980s, foreign capital was widely regarded as a threat to national sovereignty in many DCs.

In many DCs including SSACs, colonial administration has left an intense mistrust for the exploitation of domestic resources by foreign capital (Oman 1989, Meleka 1985, Akinsanya 1989). Such practices of MNCs as profit remittances, transfer pricing, etc. were widely perceived as sinister motives that undermine the national well-being of the DC involved. Therefore, many DCs have insisted on JVs with government participation where a foreign MNC is involved. With regard to SSACs, Mengistu & Haile-Mariam (1988) point out that following independence most of these countries adopted public ownership of industrial and service organizations as a matter of development policy. The restriction on foreign MNCs and the absence or infancy of private capital enabled parastatals to dominate the production and service sectors of the national economies of these countries. In some SSACs policies of indigenization of foreign firms were implemented. But this did not result to any broad based ownership, or economic benefit to the people of these countries. According to Akinsanya, the indigenization policies were generally geared to strengthen the positions of those in political power, and to help them mobilize public support.

This fear of domination by foreign MNCs, however, though strong in countries of Africa and Asia, has also been felt in other countries as well. (Artisien, Gullander 1976b, Globerman 1988). For instance, Artisien notes that in what was Yugoslavia, "..there has been an elaborate institutional and legal guarantees to protect the Yugoslav enterprise from the power of foreign multinationals". Gullander also notes that firms have encountered the impact of nationalism in venture formation across boundaries in Western European countries. Globerman, referring to OECD countries, pointed out that virtually all countries have some barriers to inward direct investment. In practical terms, the relevant question is how aggressively the formal and informal restrictions are enforced.

Though the literature does not directly relate self-reliance with joint venturing, the implication, however, is apparent. Most SSACs hold the concept of self reliance in their development objectives. (Dinham & Hines 1983). Self-reliance involves a kind of "regeneration or revitalization emanating from one's own efforts, capabilities and resources". (Max-Neef et al. 1989). But the task of economic development also increasingly requires international trade, investment, and technology transfer. (Samuelson, 1989). As Max-neef et al. indicated, therefore, self-reliance will be utterly inadequate if contained locally. 'Global' policies are required that are capable of allocating resources which further stimulate self-reliance. Self-reliance is a process defined by a system of relationships; thus becoming a process of interdependence among partners.

JVs got a boost due to the policy reviews towards privatization in many DCs during the later years of the 1980s. Though hesitant, withdrawal of the state from business activities is meant in some cases the creation of JVs between the state firms and private firms within the country, and also with foreign firms.

Some doubt, however, the trend in privatization has a solid foundation. Mengistu and Haile-Mariam (1988) argue that the recent trend in the commitment to privatization by SSACs has been not a serious one. Privatization was regarded by these countries to be an element of foreign

44

pressure by international donor agencies (AID, IBRD, IMF). Further, its objectives appear to have been misguided: emphasis has been on changing property ownership from public to private sectors, rather than making state enterprises more profitable. Besides, the authors argue that the lack of well developed infrastructure which is required for successful privatization programs, the fact that privatization of state enterprises does not necessarily bring about profitability, and as selling state enterprises to foreign interests could be interpreted as coming under neo-colonialism once again, the extent and speed of privatization in SSACs is in doubt. Other sources indicate that, though at a slower tempo, the trend in privatization in DCs including sub-Saharan Africa is progressing. The Economist (September 23, 1989), for instance, reported that there has been 600 cases of privatization world wide between 1980-1988, 400 of them in DCs, and 160 in SSACs. There is a growing awareness of the weaknesses of some of the earlier strategies for development; and of the fact that the states' role in the economy needed to be redefined (The Economist, December 9, 1989).

JVs are also considered to be relatively better for ensuring the transfer and diffusion of technology (Sethia 1988, Oates 1986). The post-investment long term benefits from the establishment of the JV is regarded highly by many host countries. From his study of JV experiences in the industries of the former Yugoslavia, Artisien has come to the conclusion that the establishment of a JV with a host partner increases the participating foreign firm's potential for purchasing raw materials and intermediate products and for servicing final markets from the host country. The multiplier effect of the JV on the economy, such as developing indigenous entrepreneurial skills and stimulating economic and service activities in the particular regions or country are among the motivations. This is evident from the case descriptions of JVs in agribusiness sector of some SSACs discussed in Chapter 2 of this book.

During the past two decades, many governments of DCs, as discussed previously, adopted a policy of encouraging private foreign investment mainly in the form of JVs to overcome their investment, economic, and technological problems, and ultimately to achieve their economic development goals. However, besides interfirm strategies, many conditions in the host country affect the decisions of firms in forming JVs. To summarize, the conditions that influence the decision of the foreign firm include: government policies on foreign ownership of investment, the socio-economic system, political stability, availability of local managerial talent and skilled manpower, extent of bureaucracy in the business culture, and the capability of the host partners.

45

Some arguments against JVs

The main problem raised against JVs is that, conflict of interest between the partners are potentially inherent in JVs than in other business involvement modes. (Freidmann and Kalmanoff, Habib & Burnett, Herzfeld 1989, Davidson). The areas of potential conflict are several, and may arise from differences in management philosophies, staffing and employment policies, interest in management control, valuation of each others contributions to the JV, exchange remittances, reinvestment of earnings/dividend distribution, local sourcing/importing, marketing locally/exporting, etc.

For these reasons, JVs are widely considered to be relatively less stable than other business forms. The high 'divorce rate' among JVs is presented as evidence as a proof of their instability. Habib and Burnett cite Harrigan's findings that between 1924 and 1985 the average success rate for JVs was only 46%, and the average life span 3.5 years. Gomes-Casseres (1987) cites, from findings of various studies, the proportion of JVs that broke-up: 70% partnerships studied by Mckinsey, and Cooper Lybrad; half of those in Harrigan's study, and a third of those in Franko's.

However, the high rate of JV break-up could be misleading. For instance, Gomes-Casseres came to the conclusion that the instability of JVs has a lot in common with other forms (e.g. wos), and only some are unique to JVs; a JV being 'a self-liquidating strategy'. Gullander (1976a) also points out that parents may go into JVs with purposes of splitting up, or, of merger later, which in any case cannot be counted against the JV strategy. Rather the strategy, as envisaged by the partners, is a success.

Among the factors that foreign firms may count against joint venturing in DCs are:

-Incompatibility of objectives: Brada (1977) notes that while the foreign partners' interests in participating in JVs are mainly micro-oriented (e.g. profits), the interests of host partner governments tend to be macro-oriented (hard currency earnings, growth, technological progress, etc.);

-The choice of host partners is limited in many DCs;

-There are pressures on foreign firms to go into JVs with parastatals while some foreign firms are reluctant to do business with governments;

46

-JVs require relatively a lot of administrative engagement and expenses;

-Local managerial and manpower placements are often influenced by nepotism; and

-Involvement in a JV may curtail flexibility; i.e. the parent foreign firm might find it difficult to take independent actions to take advantage of some business opportunities.

On the DCs side, there is little argument in the literature against JVs. One issue often raised is the disadvantages of over-emphasis given to joint venturing in general, and host majority ownership in particular. Though many foreign firms have embraced the JV strategy, there are firms that do not like to involve in JVs. And when they are involved they require majority ownership. Killing (1983), from his study of JV experiences of managers of firms in developed countries (Canadian, American and West European) came to the conclusion that "..many firms with valuable technology will not supply it to a JV in which they own less than 50%". (P.43). Franko (1987) surveyed American firms' involvement in 'new forms of investment' comparing five industries, and came to the conclusion that generally American firms taken as a group are reluctant to enter into minority or 50-50 JVs in DCs.

Therefore, the insistence on JVs and on host majority JVs could result in foregoing the benefits that accrue from foreign investment by the DC. On the other hand, studies critical of foreign investment in DCs see JVs as a strategy of the MNCs to adjust to reality. (Widstrand & Amin 1975). These studies assert that JVs generally involve only the 'self-servicing local elite', with little change in the dominant position of the MNCs or economic advantage to the host country and the general public.

Determinants of JV formation

Determinants of JV formation in general

Determinants of JV entry have been studied by Freidmann and Kalmanoff (1961), Gullander (1976b), Davidson (1982), Kogut (1988), Beamish. On a broader context, issues related to determinants of foreign direct investment flows to DCs have been studied by Tomlinson (1970), O'Sullivan (1985), Pollio and Reimenschneider (1988), Poynter (1982); and more specifically to SSACs by Agodo (1978), Afriyie (1988), and Bennell (1990).

Only Gullander and Davidson studied determinants of JVs, while others considered them as issues related to the specific problems of investigation in their studies. Kogut's work is a thorough review of existing studies on theoretical and empirical perspectives of JVs. Though he did not explain determinants directly, his study shows how various works converge on some important aspects which are the basis of determinants discussed by Gullander and Davidson.

Davidson's study, mainly based on the experiences of US based MNCs describes the strategies, i.e. the environmental and internal factors that impact upon the decision of firms in operating and expanding globally. Davidson identifies the major determinants for a company in adopting a particular strategy (from wholly owned affiliates, JVs and licensing) for participating globally to be: a) host country conditions, b) industry, c) product, and d) the firm.

From an empirical research of companies in Europe, Gullander has come up with a framework outlining the critical factors determining entry into a JV by companies. (see Fig. 3.1). In this model, Gullander identifies three groups of factors as determinants of entry into a JV: a) 'country', b) 'industry', and c) 'company'. The country factors refer to the general environment, in the form of business climate of an entire country as it affects the firm. Industry comprises of those factors that characterize a given industry, and company addresses the internal company characteristics that are decisive in launching a firm into a JV.

Obstacles are the various organizational, legal and fiscal problems which are inherent to JVs, and which are often faced by firms attempting joint venturing. The model also outlines the alternatives for achieving the expansion objective of the firm, i.e. going it alone, acquisition/merger, or joint venturing; and relates how these alternatives are influenced by other strategic decisions.

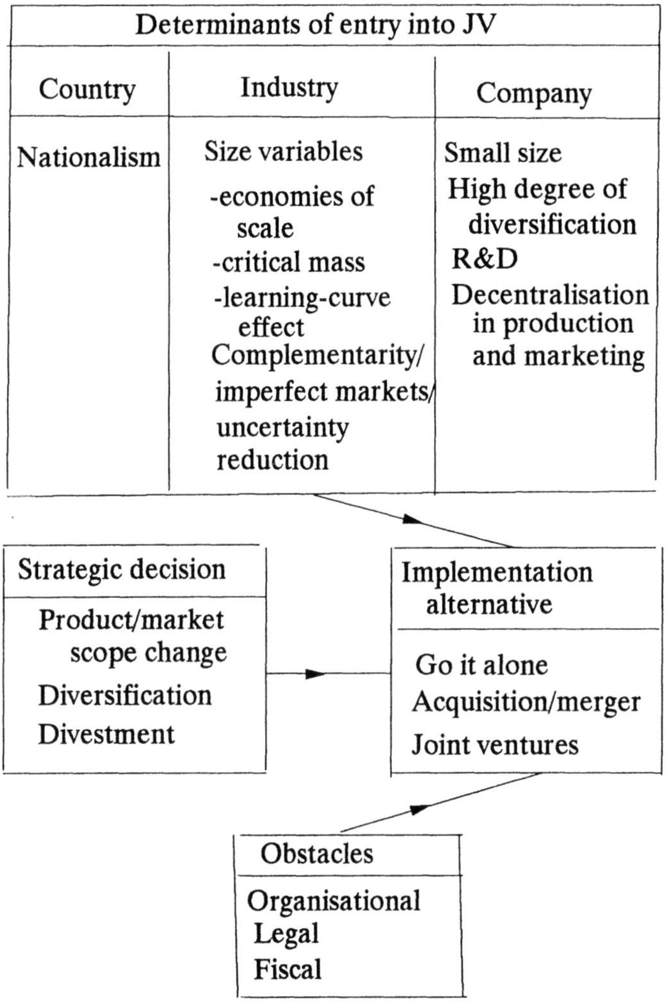

Determinants of entry into JV		
Country	Industry	Company
Nationalism	Size variables -economies of scale -critical mass -learning-curve effect Complementarity/ imperfect markets/ uncertainty reduction	Small size High degree of diversification R&D Decentralisation in production and marketing

Strategic decision	Implementation alternative
Product/market scope change Diversification Divestment	Go it alone Acquisition/merger Joint ventures

Obstacles
Organisational Legal Fiscal

Source: Gullander, 1976b. p.88.

Fig. 3.1 Determinants of joint ventures

The emphasis of Gullander's work is on the three major determinants, which were discussed under two broad sections. Under 'country and industry determinants of entry', nationalism, size, and other factors (complementarity of resources, technological strength, competition, etc.) are discussed. Under 'company determinants of entry', company size and diversification are identified as the most important individual company characteristics in determining a firm's propensity to enter a JV. Though Davidson identifies product as a separate and major determinant, Gullander has also discussed product characteristics as a component of technological and marketing conditions.

Davidson like Gullander explains that the role of the product in influencing the business strategy of the foreign firm, i.e. in choosing between a JV and other forms of business participation in a host country, is mainly influenced by the 'technology content' of the product. Davidson writes "..high technology content is generally associated with policies that emphasize complete control and ownership of foreign affiliates". (p.26). Due to the foreign firms' possession of market and bargaining power, it can effectively negotiate to go it alone, rather than involve a local partner. Therefore, both authors have reached at the same factors as determinants.

Though Gullander's model provides a useful framework for the study of JV entry determinants, some shortcomings are in evidence. The framework is constructed on the basis of experiences of ventures in European industrialized countries, and its application in a different setting is not tested. For instance, under the determinant 'country' only nationalism is discussed, which any way is not so much of a problem between European firms but which can be critically important in many DCs. In many DCs, policies and regulations impacting upon foreign participation are exercised, which are more tangible and measurable than the concept of nationalism. Another point is that the discussion is based on experiences of manufacturing firms and does not include the non-manufacturing sectors. Besides, there is reason to believe that the agribusiness sector may differ from the manufacturing sector in general, particularly when it involves DCs. Gullander himself pointed out that the framework is tentative, and further refinements are necessary by looking into different industries, and by 'a formal testing procedure'.

The wide ranging literature in reference to the research question are discussed in some detail in the following sections by adopting the framework proposed by Gullander, and organized in three sections: foreign firm specific factors, host country specific factors and food and agribusiness specific factors.

Foreign firm specific factors

Preferred strategy for business involvement: For a company the spectrum of entry to a foreign market ranges from 'export' to 'foreign production', including JVs and licensing, each associated with a certain level of risk and control over strategy (Cundiff & Hilger 1988). Though it can be assumed that wos, JVs and licensing represent the major forms, this classification seems incomplete as it does not distinguish between different categories of JVs nor considers management and technical agreements which are becoming popular and may be taken to differ from equity based JV agreements.

While most JVs between firms of developed countries are on 50-50 basis, JVs between developed country firms and developing country firms tend to be either minority or majority owned. Studies of Beamish (1988) and Reynolds (1979) indicate that in the majority of cases considered, the foreign partner was in a minority equity position while only a small proportion (less than 20% of the cases) was in the 50-50 ownership category. In developed countries JVs, the 50-50 JV category accounted for about half of the cases studied. Beamish (1988) cites Franko's findings that in 71 developing country-based JVs of 8 American firms, in none of the JVs had the firms a majority equity interest.

The reasons for the foreign firms for taking minority positions were varied. And among them, compliance with existing regulations and/or local tax advantages was the dominant reason. Other reasons noted include the foreign firms appreciation of the aspirations of DCs for local control of their national economies, and in some DCs environments the foreign firm's choice of being 'low profile'. However, the evidence from the literature whether foreign firms take minority position in a JV more from host country press or by choice is not conclusive.

Preferred host partners for JV formation: Previous studies of the characteristics of JVs in developed and DCs suggest that involvement of the government is more significant in the later countries. Many sources have generalized that foreign firms avoid state-owned firms in host countries as partners. The findings of Raveed & Renforth (1983) indicate that MNC executives favor forming JVs with local private firms over all other forms of foreign equity investment - including wos and other JV forms. Among the reasons given to why parastatals are inappropriate partners are that they cannot supply good general managers to the JV, and they also are motivated by factors other than the JVs financial returns, such as providing social benefits.

Drawing from various studies, Beamish (1985) notes that where the scale of investment was particularly high, (such as the extractive industries) or an economic sector considered crucial to the national economy, the involvement of government as partners was higher. Further, regarding the performance of such JVs, they are generally unsatisfactory. The literature on JVs indicate that identifying and selecting an appropriate partner is not only the most important undertaking, but also a difficult and time consuming affair. (Raveed & Renforth, Wright & Russell, Beamish 1988). Beamish stresses that inspite of its determining importance to success or failure, partner selection has not been given the time and attention that it deserves.

Resources and attributes expected from host partners: Resource and attribute needs of partners have been studied by Stopford and Wells (1972), Raveed and Renforth (1983), Beamish (1987). Basing on the works of the former two, Beamish develops a 'typology of need' that fall into five groups: a) items readily capitalized, b) human resource needs, c) market access needs, d) government/political needs and e) knowledge needs. Each of these groups is composed of other items. For example: items readily capitalized is explained by raw materials, capital, and technology and equipment. Knowledge needs are explained by country-related knowledge, local management and knowledge of business practices. Beamish expanded the 'need items' of partners to a total of 16.

These needs are described in general, and as already discussed previously, needs of the foreign partners and those of the host partners differ. In fact, the difference of the needs provide the complementary of the resources and attributes which is the basis of a JV. In the African country context, foreign partners would contribute resources that the host partner would generally does not possess, mainly process technology, products and access to foreign markets. Technology can be explained by machinery and equipment, and the accompanied technical skills. According to Dinham & Hines the strength of the foreign firm lies with its trademarks and brand names particularly where production is for export to developed country markets.

The host partner generally contributes country-specific assets and knowledge of the socio-cultural and political environment (Afriyie, Beamish 1985). To be specific to the agribusiness sector, the type of potential contributions of a host partner towards a JV can be summarized as: supply of raw materials, cheap labor, offices and buildings, local influence and contacts, marketing channels, finance, access to land, management/technical skills, local technology, and machinery and equipment. As can be seen from the paragraphs above, the resource needs of the host partners are scarcer than those needed by the foreign partner, hence putting the African firms in a weaker position in a partnership. An important issue for policy makers is, therefore, which are the critical resources foreign firms want, and how can these be met to attract them. As there is an indication that medium/small firms could be better in providing more appropriate technology, better meet the fragmented nature of African markets, and could also be more 'equal partners' to firms in SSACs, the size factor of the foreign partner is considered important in the study.

Host-country specific factors

Generally, a number of factors are identified in the literature that determine (as attractions or barriers) for a foreign firm to enter into a JV in a host DC. The most often mentioned factors include: political and economic instabilities, small domestic markets, lack of skilled manpower, labor costs, underdeveloped infrastructure, lack of raw materials, foreign exchange shortages, scarcity of capable partners, restrictions on profit and capital repatriations, import restrictions, risks of nationalization and expropriation.(Wright & Russell 1975, Poynter 1982, Raveed & Renforth 1983, Oman 1989, UNCTC 1988, Beamish 1987, 1985, Bennell 1990). The literature on the major factors that form the host country specific determinants are reviewed in some detail in the following paragraphs

Political factor: The political factor in the host country is considered to be a critical issue in the decision process of the foreign investor to make any investment commitment. (Beamish 1985, Hertzfeld 1991, Poynter, Greene & Villanueva 1990, Knowles & Mathur 1989, Bennell 1990). Political factors, though mentioned in the literature as an important determinant of JV formation in a DC, it is not a consistently defined concept. It is often left out of many analyses due to the difficulty in specifying the related factors and quantification (Greene & Villanueva). For instance, Knowles & Mathur note the different political environment in China as one of the problems faced by the foreign investor, without elaborating what this political environment constitutes. Nevertheless, political factors are implied in many studies to mean government policies affecting foreign investment

53

in the host country. Poynter found it useful to speak in terms of 'government intervention risks' rather than 'political risks'.

Beamish (1985) notes from Gullander's study that the primary reason for many multinational firms in less developed countries to accept the JV structure was 'political'. He cites various studies that established the importance of government policies in influencing foreign firms' decisions to form JVs in DCs. For instance, findings of Killing (1983), Jager (1980), Gullander (1976), and Tomlinson (1970) showed government 'suasion or legislation' as the major reason for most foreign firms to enter into JV agreements. In these studies, such government policies and legislations are understood to lay the 'political environment' affecting the JV process. The same relation is observed in Afriyie's study (1988). He notes that governments in DCs enacted legislation and administered investment codes for political and economic reasons. Killing (1983) points out that government insistence, i.e. the pressure on foreign firms to participate in local JVs is more pronounced in DCs.

Government policy: A UNCTC report (1988) indicated that the last decade has seen a shift in government policies of DCs in order to attract foreign direct investment. Generally, restrictive regulations of the 1960s and 1970s have given way to reducing obstacles and restrictions, and to granting guarantees and incentives. There came to be a general recognition of 'the likelihood of mutual beneficial cooperation' foreign direct investment provides.

Markets: Host country markets are among the most important determinants for foreign firms to enter into JVs (Killing 1983, Knowles & Mathur, Shenkar 1990). Killing cites Janger's findings that the most common reasons for firms to enter into JV arrangements as: to develop new markets and gain access to raw materials. In their studies of the Chinese situation, Knowles & Mathur, and Shenkar highlight the vast market potential (numerically the world's largest consumer market) as the attraction to JV formation in China. Block points out that the rush by Western companies to the former USSR for establishing JVs was mainly to seize the Soviet market of 250 million people.

Partners: As shown previously there are strong arguments given in the literature that foreign partners prefer local private firms as partners. However, the paucity of entrepreneurship in general and that of capable host partners in particular are among the many barriers that reduce the scope for JVs in DCs. Further, some foreign firms are not so willing to forego majority ownership, which might mean foregoing control and influence. Bennell's (1990) study of foreign direct investment in ESACs identified minority ownership as one of the constraints that has been faced by foreign (British) investors. Therefore, the availability of capable host partners, and their attitudes towards majority/minority ownership in a JV are important factors that need be investigated.

Incentives: Mostly, inducements by host countries took two forms: financial (tax rebates to encourage the foreign investor to re-invest, to locate the venture in less developed part of the country); and non-financial (to induce the increase in the flow of modern technology, saving foreign exchange, etc.). (Bennell, UNCTC, Artisien, Knowles & Mathur).

Among the incentives widely provided include market protection, tax and custom exemptions (tax holidays, low corporate taxes, etc.). Regarding market protection, it can be an effective policy in cases of import substituting activities, particularly where the host economy is large. Generally however, the effectiveness of such incentives in attracting foreign direct investment is not taken for granted in the literature. For instance, while low tax rates on corporate profits are provided by most DCs, their necessity and effectiveness to attract foreign investors varies from country to country and region to region (Barry 1991). Bennell's findings from his survey of British companies with investment interests in ESACs also cast doubts as to the importance of investment incentives. He found that none of the companies surveyed considered investment incentives as important for their future investment decisions.

Infrastructure: Underdeveloped infrastructure is perceived to be one of the basic constraints for increased foreign direct investment in DCs. Infrastructure is a broad concept. It is more often discussed in the 'physical' context comprising telecommunications, transportations, power and water supply. (UNCTC). It is also discussed in the 'financial' context referring to the stock exchange market and banking (Greene & Villaneuva). The importance of financial markets have been stressed by studies of Greene & Villaneuva, Knowles & Mathur and Hertzfeld. Knowles and Mathur note that the recent commencement of trading of stocks in China has been an important incentive for JVs. It has become a source of financing for JVs, and also, as mainly employees have the privilege of buying stocks, this has been a source of increased efficiency in the JV. In like manner, Hertzfeld discusses the instrumental role the stock exchange market to be created in the USSR would play in attracting, and in the eventual success of JVs.

Foreign exchange: The scarcity of foreign exchange directly affects the possibility of profit repatriation for the foreign partner. (Bennell, Smith 1987). The shortage of foreign exchange and the subsequent control would mean that profits from the JV might not be transferred to the home country of the foreign partner. Smith, drawing from his experiences with JVs spanning for a period of over 30 years, points out:

> ...When trying to establish a JV with a foreign company or individual, it is essential to understand that the forecast benefits for the foreign partner are not truly benefits until they are transmitted to the foreign partner's homeland...If it can never be returned to the (foreign partner's homeland), it loses all value to the (foreign partner)...If it cannot be returned for a decade, it has only a fraction of the value it would if it could be returned and used immediately. (pp.17-18).

Others: One of the rare studies conducted to investigate foreign direct investment in African countries is that of Bennell. His study indicates that the total British investment in African countries declined from 4.5% (of the total overseas investment) in 1978 to 0.5% in 1986. The main constraints he identified include: scarcity of foreign exchange, price controls, government bureaucracy, corruption, minority ownership, and general depressed economic conditions. Bureaucratic delays and corruption are also impending problems that discouraged JV formation in other DCs (Hertzfeld, Bennell).

The food and agribusiness sector specific factors

The problems faced by DCs to develop their agribusiness sector, the need for foreign resources, and therefore the role of JVs are discussed in Chapter 2 of this book. The unique characteristics of agribusiness, which are reviewed briefly in Chapter 1; and the reasons why it requires a different approach have been discussed by Downey and Erickson (1987), Baum and Tolbert (1985), Torok et al.(1991), Williams and Karen (1985), Amador & Starbird (1989), Glover & Kusterer (1990). Literature on the role and trend of JVs in countries of sub-Saharan Africa, and the determinants of their formation, operation, success or failure are relatively scarce. In view of the unique characteristics of agribusiness and the particular needs of prospective foreign and host partners to form JVs, two very important factors are identified: complementarity, and uncertainty reduction.

Complementarity: Some of the characteristics mentioned, i.e. the impact of government programs and policies, size of local agribusiness, family and community orientation of local agribusiness suggest that host institutions will have significant impact in the formation of JVs. Foreign firms may find it difficult to acquire land, as in most African countries this is prohibited or severely limited. The local partners could find it easier in dealing with land and farm labor questions. (Glover & Kusterer). Besides, crop and livestock production are generally in small holder sector which can be better accessed by local partners. Investing on land, hiring labor, managing farms, processing, and marketing would require not only substantial financial commitment but also close collaboration of government and other organizations which makes spreading risks worthwhile.

Food and beverage manufacturing belong to 'mature industries', exhibiting fairly standardized technologies. (Afriyie). Further, technologies in food and beverage production are widely available, and are not generally prohibitively expensive. McGee and Segal-Horn (1989) in their study of the food industry in Europe note that processing technology in the food sector has been diffusing and becoming less proprietary. Other evidences show that this is not limited to Europe, but is an international trend. Hence foreign partners who contribute products or process technologies face little or no risk of loosing a competitive edge in propriety knowledge to local partners. Therefore, foreign firms in this sector are more likely to enter into JVs with local partners than those firms in the 'technologically-intensive' industries. (Afriyie p.60). As pointed out previously, for SSACs the technology input of the foreign partners is to remain crucial, for the following reasons:

-Technology needs get more sophisticated as the stage of processing (manufacturing the food or drink product) progresses;

-Many SSACs depend on export of agricultural products, and many aspire to diversify and upgrade to high standard manufactured agricultural products for earning foreign exchange; and

-Competition in the international market place for food and drink products is highly competitive, requiring modern technology to meet the high standards.

Uncertainty reduction: Due to the characteristics inherent to agribusinesses, particularly seasonality and exposure to vagaries of nature, foreign firms could be attracted to JVs with local firms to reduce risks. Agribusiness is basically attached to land, and the land question in SSACs is a sensitive issue (Dinham & Hines, Glover & Kusterer, Akinsanya). Land ownership by foreign firms can be a basis of conflict, leading to possible expropriation.

Comments on the literature reviewed

Limitations of the prior literature

The review of the literature on the determinants of JV formation has shown the following limitations.

i)   As shown by Tomlinson, there is a lack of tangible information regarding international JVs in general, and the situation is worse in DCs. The majority of the literature focuses on interfirm relations in the economically developed countries.

ii) The limited literature on JVs in DCs are based on the experiences of the relatively more developed countries of Asia, the Middle East, and Latin America. Studies referring to countries of sub-Saharan Africa are limited. SSACs differ in a lot of ways (politically, economically and socially), and the experiences of countries of other regions may not be relevant.

     After two decades since Tomlinson's observation as pointed out under i) above, the same concern is repeated by Bennell who point out that the paucity of research attention to Africa is not only in the case of JVs, but regarding foreign direct investment in general. Bennell notes:

     ...at a time when...important policy shifts are occurring, it is surprising to find that so little substantive research is being undertaken on foreign direct investment in Africa, both in absolute terms and in relation to what was being done during the 1970. (p.156)

iii)   Studies dealing with the preference of firms from various market entry modes, i.e wos, JVs, licensing, export/import, etc. treated JVs in general without attempting to distinguish between the different types of JV alternatives: (foreign) majority JVs, co-ownership, and (foreign) minority JVs. As majority JV generally implies management control of the venture, it is important to identify the attitudes of the prospective partners.

iv)   Foreign firm partners are described generally as MNCs. No study of JV has attempted to differentiate among these firms about their attitudes towards joint venturing.

v)   Studies that dealt with entry determinants did not attempt to identify the relative importance of major factors.

vi)   Studies on JVs emphasize the manufacturing sector. Albeit the important role of agribusiness in the economies of DCs, very little attention is given to the sector in the JV literature.

A Review of the framework

As a summary of the literature review, and to construct a framework to guide primary data gathering, Gullander's model (1976b) is adopted for this study after some adjustments. In the framework proposed by Gullander and cited previously in this chapter, major determinants are identified as 'country', 'industry', and 'company'. From the literature review discussed in the previous sections of this chapter, and the limitations highlighted above, the framework can be enriched by incorporating more specific elements to better guide the conduct of the study. The changes made are as follows:

i)   'Country' is changed to host country specific entry environment. Nationalism is found to be vague and difficult to measure in a survey. Instead, government policy, and attitudes of policy makers are used.

ii) '*Industry*' is changed to the specific sector of this study: the food and agribusiness sector. Industry determinants are outlined as size (comprising economies of scale, critical mass and learning-curve effect), complementarity in resources, competence between partners, imperfect market conditions, and uncertainty reduction. Taken in the context of international JV formation between firms from the developed economies and firms from a DC in the agribusiness sector, the major determinants would differ at least in one aspect.

The size factor, as described by Gullander, is more relevant where the firms are engaged in standardized products with a continuous market, such as chemicals, drugs, plastics, trucks, etc. Davidson explains standardized products as those products whose production is generally characterized by capital intensive, volume-oriented facilities for world wide markets, and are exemplified as in electronics, automobile, steel, etc. In applying the framework in a sector which is broader than a specific industry involving companies operating in one or a combination of various activities (agri-production, processing, manufacturing, distribution, marketing, and services) the size factor relevant is the extent of the firms resources that enables it to undertake international participation effectively. Generally, such size categories are based on assets, turnover, or number of employees.

Therefore, the emphasis in the model adopted for this study focuses on size as defined above, the partner needs and complementarity of resources, competence of partners, and risk reduction factors. Further, the strategic choice of business outlined in Gullander's model, go-it-alone, JVs, and acquisition/merger is modified to include the whole range of alternatives: from wos to import/export.

iii) '*Company*': The firms of interest for the study are defined as UK based food and agribusiness firms with business interest in SSACs. The internal characteristics of firms is not the primary concern of this study. The focus is on their strategy with regard to business involvement in SSACs. Therefore, firm specific factors for the study are: choice of business involvement strategy, choice among host partners, their need for critical resources, and the perceived obstacles in the host country that impede their entry into a JV.

Filling the gap identified in this literature review requires data that need to be gathered in SSACs and within the UK. The nature of data to be gathered from the UK, measuring and understanding the opinions and attitudes of decision makers in the agribusiness firms, suggest that a survey of senior executives is appropriate. On the other hand, the data required to explain the business environment in the SSACs context is too broad and difficult to be tackled through a survey. Authors experienced in studying African affairs (e.g. Killick 1992, Loutfi) have expressed their dismay with regard to the problems of inadequate data, and when some data is available its reliability. The present researcher also had to encounter the same problems.

In such circumstances, where the nature of enquiry is basically exploratory, the case study strategy is more appropriate. As discussed previously, SSACs and JV formation in the agribusiness sector are not well covered in the literature and there is a need for a pilot study to be able to define variables and concepts more sharply before launching the survey or the case study.

References

Afriyie, K.(1988). 'Factor Choice Characteristics and Industrial Impact of Joint Ventures: Lessons From a Developing Economy', *Columbia Journal of World Business.* vol.23 no.2. pp.51-61.

Agodo, O. (1978). 'The Determinants of US Private Manufacturing Investments in Africa', *Journal of International Business.* vol.10. Winter. pp.95-107.

Akinsanya, A.A.(1989). 'Economic Nationalism in Africa: Illusion and Reality', *TransAfrica Forum.* vol.6 no.2. pp.49-60.

Amador R.E. & Starbird, S.A.(1989). 'The Evaluation of International Agribusiness Investment Locations Using Multidimensional Scaling', *Agribusiness.* vol.5 no.2. pp.139-51.

Artisien, P.F.R.(1985). *Joint Ventures in Yugoslav Industry.* Gower Publishing Co. Ltd.

Auster, E.R.(1987). 'International Corporate Linkages: Dynamic Forms in Changing Environments', *The Columbia Journal of World Business.* vol.22 no.2. pp.3-6.

Barry, F.(1991). 'Industrialisation Strategies for Developing Countries: Lessons from the Irish Experience', *Development Policy Review.* vol.9 no.1 pp.85-98.

Baum, W.C. & Tolbert, S.M. (1985). *Investing in Development: Lessons of World Bank Experience*. New York: Oxford University Press.

Beamish, P.W.(1988). *Multinational Joint Ventures in Developing Countries*. Dorset: Routledge.

_____, (1987). 'Joint Ventures in Less Developed Countries: Partner Selection & Performance', *Management International Review*. vol.27 no.1. pp.23-37.

_____, (1985). 'The Characteristics of Joint Ventures in Developed and DCs', *Columbia Journal of World Business*. vol.20 no.3. pp.13-9.

Bennel, P.(1990). 'British Industrial Investment in sub-Saharan Africa: Corporate Responses to Economic Crisis in 1980's', *Development Policy Review*. vol.8 no.2. pp.155-77.

Block, P.M.(1987). 'Glasnost Eases the Way for Soviet Joint Venture', *Chemical Week*. vol.141 no.21. pp.32-6.

Brada, J.C.(1977). ,Markets, Property Rights, & the Economics of Joint Ventures in Socialist Countries', *Journal of Competitive Economics*. vol.1 part 2. pp.167-81.

Cavusgil, S.T. & Ghauri, P.N.(1990). *Doing Business in Developing Countries: Entry and Negotiation Strategies*. London: Routledge.

Chen. E.K.Y.(ed.) (1990). *Foreign Direct Investment in Asia*. Tokyo: Asia Productivity Organization.

Cohen, J.A.(1982). 'Equity Joint Ventures: 20 Pitfalls that Every Company Shall Know About', *The China Business Review*. November-December pp.26-30.

Connoly, S.G.(1984). 'Joint Ventures With Third World Multi-nationals: a New Form of Entry to International Markets', *Columbia Journal of World Business*. vol.19 no.2. pp.18-22.

Cundiff, E.W. & Hilger, M.T.(1988). *Marketing in the International Environment*. Prentice Hall. 2nd Edition.

Davidson, W.H.(1982). *Global Strategic Management*. New York: John Wiley and Sons.

Dawson, L.M.(1987). 'Transferring Industrial Technology to Less Developed Countries', *Industrial Marketing Management*. vol.16 no.4. pp.265-71.

Dinham, B. & Hines, C. (1983). *Agribusiness in Africa*. London: Earth Resources Research Ltd.

Dodwell, D.(1992). 'Investors Avoiding Cheap-labour States', *Financial Times*. May 21. p.8.

Downey, W.D. & Erickson, S.P.(1987). *Agribusiness Management*. McGraw-Hill. 2nd Edition.

Eales, R.(1990). 'Joint Ventures: Partners for Richer or Poorer', *The Independent on Sunday.* 18 March. p.28.

'Economics Brief: the Bleak Continent', *The Economist.* December 9, 1989. pp.100-101.

Franko, L.G.(1987). 'New Forms of Investment in Developing Countries by US Companies: a Five Industries Comparison', *The Columbia Journal of World Business.* vol.22 no.2. pp.39-55.

George, S.(1977). *How the Other Half Dies: the Real Reason for World Hunger.* Penguin Books.

Globerman, S.(1988). 'Government Policies Towards Foreign Direct Investment: Has a New Era Dawned?', *The Columbia Journal of World Business.* vol.23 no.3. pp.41-9.

Glover, D. & Kusterer, K.(1990). *Small Farmers, Big Business.* Houndmills: the MacMillan Press Ltd.

Goldenberg, S.(1989). *International Joint Ventures in Action.*

Gomes-Casseres, B.(1987). 'Joint Venture Instability: Is it a Problem', *The Columbia Journal of World Business.* vol.22 no.2. pp.97-101.

Greene, J. and Villaneuva, D.(1990). 'Determinants of Private Investment in Less Developed Countries', *Finance & Development.* December. pp.40-2.

Gullander, S.(1976a). 'Joint Ventures and Corporate Strategy', *Columbia Journal of World Business.* vol.11 no.1 Spring. pp.104-14.

_____, (1976b). 'Joint Ventures in Europe: Determinants of Entry', *International Studies of Management and Organizations.* vol.1-2 no.6. Spring-Summer. pp.85-111.

Habib, G.M. & Burnett, J.J.(1989). 'An Assessment of Channel Behaviour in an Alternative Structural Arrangement: the International Joint Venture', *International Marketing Review.* vol.6 no.3. pp.7-21.

Harrigan, K.R.(1988). 'Joint Ventures and Competitive Strategy', *Strategic Management Journal.* vol.9 no.2. pp.141-58.

_____, (1987). 'Strategic Alliances: Their New Role in Global Competition', *The Columbia Journal of World Business.* vol.22 no.2. pp.67-9.

_____, (1986). *Managing for Joint Venture Success.* Lexington: Heath & Co.

Harrison, J.S.(1987). 'Alternatives to Merger: Joint Ventures and Other Strategies', *Long Range Planning.* vol.20. no.6. pp.78-83.

Hertzfeld, J.M.(1991). 'Joint Ventures: Saving the Soviets From Perestroika', *Harvard Business Review.* January-February. pp.80-91.

Herzfeld, E.(1989). *Joint Ventures.* 2nd edition. Jordans.

Kent, D.H.(1991). 'Joint Ventures vs. Non-Joint Ventures: an Empirical Investigation', *Strategic Management Journal.* vol.12. pp.387-93.

Killick, T.(1992). 'Explaining Africa's Post-Independence Development Experiences', *ODI Working Paper 60.* ODI: London.

Killing, J.P.(1983). *Strategies for Joint Venture Success.* Croom Helm Ltd.

_____ (1980). 'Technology Acquisition: License Agreement or Joint Ventures', *The Columbia Journal of World Business.* Fall. pp.38-47.

Knowles, L.L. and Mathur, I.(1989). 'Joint Venture Strategies for Marketing in China', *Journal of International Consumer Marketing.* vol.2 no.1. pp.37-54.

Kogut, B.(1988). 'Joint Ventures: Theoretical and Empirical Perspectives', *Strategic Management Journal.* vol.9. pp.319-32.

Loutfi, M.(1989). 'Development Issues and State Policies in sub-Saharan Africa', *International Labor Review.* vol.128 no.2. pp. 137-53.

Max-Neef, M. et al.(1989). 'Development & Self-reliance', *Development Dialogue 1989:* 1. Uppsala: The Dag Hammerskjold Foundation. pp. 54.

McGee J. & Segal-Horn, S.(1989). 'Changes in the European Food Processing Industry: the Consequences of 1992', *Working Paper SWP 29/89.* Cranfield: Cranfield School of Management.

Meadley, J.(1989). A More Significant Role for the Private Sector in Agricultural Development. (unpublished monograph).

Meleka, A. H.(1985). 'The Changing Role of Multinational Corporations', *Management International Review.* vol.25 no.1. pp.36-45.

Mengistu, B. & Haile-Mariam, Y.(1988). 'The State & Future of Privatization in Sub-Saharan Africa', *Journal of African Studies,* vol.15 no.1&2. Spring/Summer. pp.4-9.

Najafbagy, R.(1985). 'Operations of Multinational Corporations and Local Enterprise in Arab Countries', *Management International Review.* vol.25 No.4. pp.46-57.

Oates, D.(1986). 'Enterprise: the New China syndrome', *Director.* vol.40 no.3. October. pp.36-9.

Oman, C.(1989). *New Forms of Investment in Developing Country Industries.* Paris: OECD.

O'Sullivan, P. (1985). 'Determinants and Impact of Private Foreign Direct Investment in Host Countries', *Management International Review.* vol.25 no.1. pp.28-35.

Pollio, G. & Riemenschneiner, C.H.(1988). 'The Coming Third World Investment Revival', *Harvard Business Review.* March-April. vol.66 no.2. pp.114-24.

'Poor Man's Burden: A Survey of the Third World', *The Economist,* September 23, 1989. (Survey section pp.1-58).

Poynter, T.A.(1982). 'Government Intervention in Less Developed Countries: the Experience of Multinational Companies', *Journal of International Business Studies.* Spring-Summer. pp.9-25.

Raveed, S.R. & Renforth, W.(1983). 'Sate Enterprise-Multinational Corporation Joint Ventures: How Well Do They Meet Both Partners' Needs?', *Management International Review.* vol. 1 Part 1. pp.47-57.

Samuelson, R.J.(1989). 'Capitalism and Freedom', *NewsWeek,* June 12. p.6.

Sethia, N.(1988). 'From Regulation to Innovation: Emerging Trends in India', *New Management.* vol.6 no.2. pp.32-6.

Shenkar, O.(1990). 'International Joint Ventures' Problems in China: Risks and Remedies', *Long Range Planning.* vol.23 no.3. pp.82-90.

Smith, C.H.(1987). *Negotiating and Managing Joint Ventures: Lessons from Practical Experience.* Geneva: International Labor Organization.

Stoever, W.A.(1989). 'Why State Corporations in Developing Countries Have Failed to Attract Foreign Investment', *International Marketing Review.* vol.6 no.3. pp.62-78.

Stopford, J.M. & Wells, L.T.(Jr.) (1972). *Managing the Multinational Enterprise.* New York: Basic Books.

Tomlinson, J.1970). *The Joint Venture Process in International Business: India and Pakistan.* MIT Press.

Torok, S.J. et al. (1991). Management Assistance Needs of Small Food and Kindred Products Processors. *Agribusiness.* vol.7 no.5. pp.447-61.

UNCTC (1988). *Transnational Corporations in World Development: Trends and Prospects.* New York: United Nations.

Widstrand, C. & Amin, S.(1975) (ed.). *Multinational Firms in Africa.* Uppsala: Scandinavian Institute of African Studies.

Williams, S. & Karen, R.(1985). *Agribusiness and the Small-scale Farmer.* Westview Press.

Wright, R.W. and Russell, C.S.(1975). 'Joint Ventures in Developing Countries: Realities and Responses', *Columbia Journal of World Business.* Summer. pp.74-80.

4 Methodology: Research design, data collection and analysis

Introduction

This chapter discusses the research design and the procedures of data collection and analysis. In reviewing the determinants of joint venture (JV) formation in the previous chapter, it was noted that collection of data in the UK as well as in African countries would be necessary. It was also pointed out that since the research problem is concerned with countries of sub-Saharan Africa and JV formation in the agribusiness sector, none of which were covered adequately in the previous literature, launching a pilot study was found essential. Therefore in this chapter, the methodological framework and procedures are discussed.

The chapter has 6 parts including introduction. In the research design section, the types of data required, the instruments of data collection, and the reasons for using the two major research strategies i.e., the case study and the survey are outlined briefly. In the subsequent three sections details of procedures for conducting the pilot study, the case study and the survey are discussed with their respective data collection instruments. Finally, the method of data analysis and the reasons why non-parametric techniques were found appropriate for testing the hypotheses are discussed.

Research design

According to Dooley (1984) and Krausz and Miller (1974) all research can generally be classified into either qualitative or quantitative. In quantitative research the measurements and findings can be quantified while in qualitative research they are descriptive. Quantitative research covers two broad classes of research method: experimental and correlational. The experimental approach can be applicable where the researcher is able to manipulate one variable and assess the corresponding changes in another variable. The correlational methods make use of systematic observations of the relations between variables which can be measured but not manipulated. Correlational designs are further categorized into longitudinal: where observations are made on variables over some longer time period; and cross-sectional: where data are gathered at one point in time. (Walizer & Wienir 1978).

To tackle the research problem outlined for this study both qualitative and quantitative data were required, and such data needed be collected in UK and African countries. For the gathering of data from UK based company executives a questionnaire survey approach was found more appropriate. As pointed out by Bennett (1986), the survey approach is relatively cheaper, quicker and enables broader coverage. Further, using the survey method facilitates the application of statistical techniques for rigorous analysis, through testing hypotheses and making statistical generalizations. The survey research at hand, therefore, belongs to the correlational, and cross-sectional category.

Where the particular nature of the enquiry is exploratory, and where the researcher seeks to collect and examine as many data as possible regarding the subject of study, however, case study approach is considered appropriate. (Babbie 1973, Bennett). For the section dealing with African countries, therefore, where little is known with regard the JV phenomena, and where various sources of information have to be consulted the method chosen is a case study approach. In applying the two research approaches, various types of data were collected: a) secondary data; b) primary data through an experience (pilot) study, c) primary data through a survey, and d) primary and secondary data through a case study.

Secondary data were collected to compile and explain the JV phenomena, JV experiences in various DCs, characteristics of the food and agribusiness sector in sub-Saharan African countries (SSACs), and characteristics of UK based food and agribusiness companies. Secondary data collected from various published sources were supplemented by an experience (pilot) study and a review of case descriptions of agribusiness JVs in SSACs.

Primary data collection constituted the main purpose of the field study. Data were gathered through a survey of executives of UK based food and agribusiness firms with investment and trading relations with English speaking African countries (ESACs). Another set of primary data were collected through a case study of Zimbabwe. Instruments used for data collection were: a) an interview guide (for the pilot study), b) a case study protocol (for the case study of Zimbabwe), c) a mail questionnaire (for the survey of UK executives), and d) an interview schedule (for the follow-up of the questionnaire survey). The following sections present details of the methodology applied for data collection, procedures of conducting the pilot study, the case study, the survey, and analysis of the data.

Pilot study

In concluding the literature review in Chapter 3, the need to conduct a pilot study has been indicated. As SSACs and JV formation in the agribusiness sector have received little attention, a pilot survey would help to define variables and concepts more sharply for the survey and case study. For instance, it is important to find out if executives have the same understanding of the 'JV' phrase, and how they understand the regional aspect of their business interest in Africa. African countries are described in different ways in many studies, such as Africa in general, sub-Saharan Africa, Black Africa, Commonwealth members of African countries, eastern and southern African states, etc. Further, as the variables explaining determinants of JV formation are often identified in the context of the 'manufacturing' sector, it is important to verify them for the agribusiness sector.

Ten executives of UK based agribusiness firms who are known to have various business interests, including JVs in SSACs were identified and interviewed. An interview guide was used to gather data through an indepth interview of the executives. (see Appendix D). Data so collected were the basis for defining the context of the study, selection of an African country for the case study, verifying variables, and developing the instruments for primary data collection.

Case study

The case study strategy

Tackling the research problem identified for this study required documentation and analysis of the JV environment in the African country

68

setting. The alternative methods commonly used for collecting data are surveying and case study. The distinguishing features of a case study are: a) it is an empirical inquiry, b) investigates a contemporary phenomenon within its real life context, c) multiple sources of evidence are used. (Yin P.23). A definition of a case study, given by Mitchell and cited by Smith (1990) states: "a detailed examination of an event (or series of related events) which the analyst believes exhibits (or exhibit) the operation of some identified general theoretical principle". (p.14)

The strength and weakness of the case study strategy has been a subject of debate among authors in social research methodologies. The case study strategy is often criticized for lack of validity and reliability. (e.g. see Bennett). But others like Yin, Miles and Huberman (1984), and Smith do not agree. They point out that the criticisms are either prejudices or misconceptions of the method. They argue that generalization depends on cogency of theoretical reasoning, and therefore, logical inferences and not statistical inferences should apply. In other words, generalization is made to theory, not to population, and it is analytical, and not statistical.

In this study, an attempt has been made to apply tactics that would enhance the validity and reliability of the study. In particular, a case study protocol was prepared prior to the field study. (Appendix B). Data were collected from various sources, and a pattern matching approach of data analysis has been applied.

Yin identifies four types of designs in the case study strategy: single-case (holistic) designs, single-case (embedded) designs, multiple-case (holistic) designs, and multiple-case (embedded) designs. The primary distinction in a design is between single case and multiple case designs. To address the research questions of a study a single-case or multiple-cases may be used. The next decision to be made is whether the study involves more than one unit of analysis. If the study examines a single unit of analysis, then the design is 'holistic'. But if the investigation involves more than one units of analysis the design is 'embedded'.

For this study, the data were to be gathered in one country and the ensuing generalization was to be made from these data; therefore lending to a single case. Data to be gathered were in the form of opinions and attitudes of executives of various organizations, as well as published and unpublished information on some variables explaining the business environment. The several variables or issues lend to multiple units of analysis. The main units of analysis are: government policy, host partners, barriers to JV formation, and opportunities for JV formation. Therefore, the design belongs to the 'type 2', i.e., 'single-case (embedded) design' type.

Selecting a country for case study

Though the case study could have been undertaken in any one or more SSACs, countries of extreme economic and political characteristics were not considered. Selecting a country/ies of 'average' status on the basis of such characteristics as population size, GDP, and importance of agribusiness in the economy was thought to be useful to be able to draw more realistic and widely applicable conclusions from the findings.

Other criteria considered were the practical aspect of conducting research in the particular country and the level of financial resource available for the study. Viewed against these broad criteria, the final focus of attention was placed on Ghana, Ivory Coast, Kenya, Tanzania, Zambia and Zimbabwe. As Kenya is among the few African countries where various agribusiness JVs are known to operate, and as the researcher had some knowledge of the country from a previous visit, it was of primary target for the case study. However, the effort to obtain a travel and a research permit to Kenya was not successful mainly for reasons related to the political problems in the neighboring countries of Ethiopia and Somalia.

Considerable resource and time was spent to develop contacts and secure enabling conditions for research in one or two of the other countries mentioned, but only the Zimbabwe option was successful. Besides identifying and developing contacts with some JVs and some reliable informants, material conditions to facilitate the study, such as an office, telephone and word processing services could be arranged in Zimbabwe. Therefore, given the limited time and financial resources, a single case study design has been adopted for the study.

Generally, there may be doubts as to the validity of generalizing from a single case study. However, as discussed previously in this chapter, Yin, Mitchell and Miles and Huberman have explained how generalization is permissible from a single case study. That is, generalizations are made to theory and not to a population. Therefore, generalization from the findings were made to the JV formation theoretical proposition posited prior to the field work in Zimbabwe, which is discussed in the case study protocol.

The case study protocol

A protocol is a plan that guides the researcher for the a case study. In a complete protocol, the researcher outlines, an overview giving the background of the study, field procedures, the case study questions, and a guide for the case study report. The use of a well prepared protocol to enhance the reliability of the case study research is strongly recommended. (e.g. Yin). Therefore, considerable time and effort has been exerted to prepare a protocol prior to the field study of Zimbabwe. The case study protocol prepared to guide the study of Zimbabwe organized into 4 sections is given as Appendix B.

The survey

Alternatives available for gathering information through a questionnaire in a survey include: personal interviews, telephone interviews, mail interviews and computer interviews. Of these, personal interviews and mail interviews (mail questionnaires) are the most commonly used. Both methods have advantages one over the other. Personal interviews are generally characterized with more reliability of information, high response rates, more flexibility as their strength; and with being relatively expensive, susceptible for potential interviewer bias, and taking longer period of time as their weakness. Mail interviews are generally preferred to cover wide geographic area, can provide standardized responses and generally cost less; but the response rate could be low, they require limited length and complexity of questions, and there is limited control over who completes the questionnaire. (Chernatony 1988, Barabba 1990). As regards to validity and reliability, the literature indicates that it is generally difficult to choose one from the other on these basis, and therefore, choosing one of the methods would depend on the specific purpose of the survey (Gatlung, 1969, Fink & Kosecoff 1985).

In this case, where the questionnaires are addressed to company executives using the mail interview approach alone could result into too few responses. The questions refer to company policies and operations, and therefore could be regarded as sensitive; and the questionnaire had to be fairly lengthy, thereby demanding on their busy schedules. On the other hand, the personal interview alternative have its own shortcomings. Personal interviews to be administered by the researcher alone would require too long a period of time, and the cost will also be very high. Therefore, a combination of personal interview and mail questionnaire methods were considered more appropriate.

Questionnaire design

A questionnaire was prepared and used to gather data on the opinions and attitudes of Executives of UK based agribusiness firms. (Appendix C). The questions were generated based on the objectives outlined and checked against questionnaires of similar studies. (e.g. Artisien 1985). As most issues raised by the questionnaire were basically policy matters the respondents were expected to be senior executives. As such respondents were known to be economical about their time caution has been taken in preparing the questionnaire. The questionnaire was kept as short as possible, only relevant questions were asked, and alternative replies were provided to facilitate completion.

Among the scaling techniques used in attitude surveys semantic differential scale and Likert scale are the most widely used techniques (Weisberg & Bowen 1977, Tull & Hawkins). Tull and Hawkins further note that various scaling techniques provided 'equivalent results', and suggest that generally the use of multiple scales is advisable. Edris and Meidan (1990) also point out that the reliability of standard attitude scales (Thurstone, Guttman, Likert, and semantic differential scales) are generally highly reliable. Holmes (1974) points out that 5-point scales are generally most effective and easier to comprehend from the respondents point of view. Taking into consideration such factors as the type of information needed and the characteristics of the respondents, using a Likert like 5-point scale was found appropriate. However, other scales were also used depending on their appropriateness to each specific information sought.

Pretesting the questionnaire

A pretest of the questionnaire was conducted with five senior executives from five UK based agribusiness firms. The purpose was to find out how effective the questionnaire would be to collect data for the study. Therefore, the executives were asked to complete the questionnaire, and then to give their opinions and suggestions with regard the content, form, clarity and length of the questionnaire. Each question, and the response made by the test respondents were discussed item by item by the researcher and each individual respondent. Generally, the executives were happy with the questionnaire and, the several minor changes they proposed were duly considered.

Among their comments was the importance of identifying the particular respondent in an organization. As most firms were large with various operations and, therefore, involving several senior executives it would be important to identify a) the unit, department, or subsidiary dealing with the subject matter of the study, and b) the particular respondent. This has been well taken and with a few exceptions the mailing of questionnaires was done after prior contacts have been made.

Mailing package

The mail package contained i) a cover letter, ii) a note containing definitions of the JV concept and 'African countries', iii) a map showing African countries of interest, iv) the questionnaire and v) a prepaid return envelop. (Appendix C).

i) The cover letter was prepared explaining the purpose of the study, the significance of its findings in promoting business between the UK and the particular African countries through JVs. It also highlighted the importance of the views of executives in solving current business problems in African countries, and the confidentiality of the information provided. The letters were addressed to the appropriate executive by name as in most cases such executives have been priorly identified through direct telephone enquiry.

Further, as firms may have 'registered office' addresses and 'trading' addresses, the proper address of the named executive was ascertained. The positions of the respondents were varied, and included: the Managing Directors, International Operations Managers, Marketing Directors, Directors for Africa, Investment and Project Directors, etc. Allowing 7 days after mailing, the telephone follow-up would begin to know the status of the questionnaire. In some cases where the questionnaire was said not to have been received, a second letter enclosing the package has been sent.

ii) A map of Africa in which the countries of interest, ie, ESACs were marked was attached to the letter. A note was added explaining that the term 'African countries' in the questionnaire meant ESACs as shown on the map.

iii) As understandings of the term JV by different executives may vary, it was found essential to include a definition of a JV, so that the executives and the researcher have a common concept of the JV phenomenon.

iv)   The questionnaire, containing 8 questions in 6 pages was the major enclosure.

v)   A prepaid envelop with return address of the Marketing and Business Management Department was also enclosed.

All the materials were prepared on quality A4 size paper with quality print. To identify the completed questionnaire a prerecorded code corresponding to the specific firm was put on each return envelop and also inside the questionnaire. The cover letter was on white, headed paper; the map on green, and the questionnaire on yellow paper. Different colors were thought to attract attention and would also help in quick sorting and handling the different contents by the respondents. Though some sources dispute the advantage of printing on colored paper, (e.g. Dillon et al. 1990, Chernatony 1988), there was evidence in this study that it was a good strategy. During the follow-up calls made by the researcher, the questionnaire was referred to as the 'yellow papers', which in subsequent calls the executives identified the color with the questionnaire. It is believed that the color reminded the executives of the questionnaire, and might have helped them to easily identify it from the piles of papers on their desks.

Research population

Among the primary concerns in carrying out a survey research is defining and locating the research population. The research population of interest was defined as 'executives of UK based food and agribusiness firms with business interests in ESACs'. Though thorough search has been made, a list containing these firms was not available. Therefore, over the duration of the research period upto the survey, a list of such firms has been compiled from various sources. The following procedure has been used to develop the population from which a sample was to be selected and to which the generalization from the result of the survey was to be made.

i)   A list of UK-based food and beverage processing companies (MNCs) were compiled from UNCTC (1981).

ii)   A list of UK-based companies 'among the world's 100 largest food companies' were compiled from Oman (1989).

iii)   An initial list comprising 72 companies, mainly large MNCs, was prepared.

iv)   UK companies exporting food products to ESACs were identified from the Freight Information Services (FIS) Directory and added to the list. (Exporter List, FIS 1991).

v)   UK companies importing food products from ESACs were identified and added to the list. (Macleod, 1991, British Importers).

vi)   The list was edited and enlarged by sorting and checking: repetitions were excluded; more companies with 'British interests' in various ESACs were identified from the records of the Department of Trade and Industry (DTI) and were included to the list (Companies with British Interests 1990/91); more companies were identified from Dinham & Hines (1983), Maya & Tangoona (1989), the Tropical Growers Association Annual Report (1990) and added to the list.

vii)   Information regarding names of executives, addresses, turnover, number of employees, etc. were searched from various sources, including: the 'FAME' database, Key British Enterprises, Best of British, Britain's Top Privately Owned Companies, European Food Trades Directory: UK, Directory of British Consultants Bureau, Who Owns Whom UK, Kompas, the Grocer, Financial Times, and other sources.

viii)   The above procedures resulted in a data-base of firms describing them in 10 characteristics: company name, the pertinent executive's name and his/her designation, postal address and telephone number, yearly turnover, number of employees, value of annual exports, value of annual imports, classification by size, and classification by status of business position in ESACs.

ix)   Known subsidiaries were sorted and arranged separately to avoid confusion and double counting with parent firms.

x)   A final list containing details of 141 core companies which have investment, and/or trading interests in ESACs has been prepared. This was used as a working population for the survey.

Sampling design

Samples are classified into two generic types: probability samples and non-probability or purposive samples. A probability sample is where all members of the population have a known chance of selection; and where this condition is not met, the sample is classified as non-probability sample. To be able to produce statistically valid estimates the sample design adopted for the survey was a probability sample.

There are three basic options in choosing among probability sample designs: simple random sampling, stratified sampling, and cluster sampling. (Dillon et al.). Simple random sampling, while advantageous in terms of ease of data analysis, and limiting possible classification errors, its disadvantages include in not making use of knowledge of the population which the researcher might have (Miller 1983). On the other hand, stratified sampling is used where the population is divided in sub-groups. Stratified sampling provides the smallest sampling error and hence the most information for the available resources. (Sudman 1983). Cluster sampling is where "..a sample of clusters is first selected and then a decision on which sampling units to include in the sample is made" (Dillon et al.).

Pre-survey information known about the population does not allow to formulate meaningful and distinct strata. Though it is known that some companies have direct investment interests and some are involved in trading, i.e. in import/export, these characteristics are not distinct to any group of firms, and may overlap. As Dillon et al. point out, the efficiency of stratified sampling is directly tied to the efficacy of the variable used to classify the sampling units into strata; and therefore in this case, stratification was not found to be appropriate. The simple random sampling design was found more appropriate for the survey.

Due to the specialized nature of the information to be collected, the relatively small number of food and agribusiness firms that have business interest in ESACs, and the survey being limited to firms in one country, i.e. UK, covering 1/4 of the working population, i.e. about 35 usable questionnaires, was taken as the target for this survey. To extract richer information for explanatory analysis, it was planned to conduct a follow-up interview with about one-third of the respondents completing the questionnaire. Though meticulous pre-mailing preparation and follow-up were to be made, expected response rate was conservatively put at 50%. Therefore, questionnaires were mailed to 70 firms. All the firms in the population were assigned a number, and 70 numbers (70 firms) were selected at random.

Follow-up interviews

The analysis of the data gathered by the questionnaire (i.e., central tendency, measures of association, etc.) mainly answers the 'what' questions raised by the research. It fails to fully identify why executives had that particular attitude. To fill the gap, 12 interviews with executives were completed in addition to the questionnaire. An interview schedule was prepared and used. (Appendix E). The interviews were administered after the executives have completed the questionnaire. Through a quick 'eye-balling' the researcher studied the pattern of the response and asked the respondent why he (all interviewees were males) had responded in the manner. The replies were duly noted during the interview, and refined immediately afterwards while the memory of the interview was still fresh. The information thus gathered were used to explain the conclusions drawn from the statistical analyses.

Response rate

Response rates differ widely: where there are instances of 70% or more (Chernatony 1989) or even 80% or more (Dillon et al.), they can also be as low as 10%. (Barabba). The difference is said to lie mainly on the planning and preparation to secure the cooperation of the would be respondents. Prior notification, personalization, and follow-up letters are said to have positive impact on response rates, while cover letter, anonymity, inclusion of dead-line date, return postage and appeals are not effecting impact.(Dillon et al.).

However, where the respondents are senior company executives the importance of such components as cover letter, anonymity and length of questionnaire as facilitators of response cannot be ignored. For instance, questionnaire length is disputed as a facilitator for high response rate (e.g. Dillon et al., Chernatony). But, there was evidence during the survey that executives showed preference for shorter questionnaires. During premailing telephone contacts, some executives asked 'how long' the questionnaire was, and they felt reassured when told it was 'brief'. During the follow-up interview with an executive, he said rather jokingly that "next time you want me to complete a questionnaire, this (pointing at the questionnaire) should be shortened by half and then by half"!.

A total of 54 firms responded in one way or other, giving response rate of 77%. The sample included some firms whose current involvement in ESACs were not known, and the purpose of their inclusion was to know if they are involved at present and if not why. This was followed up by telephone interview. The response rate considering only the usable questionnaires was 53%. Some firms failed to complete the questionnaire, and the reasons given are summarized as shown on Table 4.1.

Table 4.1
Reasons given by some firms for not completing the questionnaire

Reasons stated	No. of firms
Company policy of:	
-not completing questionnaires	5
-not giving out company information	3
Investment decisions made at H.Q., not in UK	2
No policy of JVs	1
Lack of time & resources	3
No current/future interest in ESACs	3
Total	17

Determining groups based on size

In studies of international business little distinction is made between large and smaller MNCs. Yet, in dealing with international business relations with ESACs, medium/small firms of developed countries would be of importance in two aspects, as discussed in a UNCTC report (1988): a) considering the various measures used in different countries, the small transnational enterprises accounted for over half of the firms with investment abroad; and b) small and medium-size TNCs might be particularly suitable partners for the low-income countries. It was implied that DCs might attain better success in their search for products and technologies for their development objectives from medium/small TNCs. Table 4.2 shows, for five of the countries that account for the major share of foreign investment in the world, the basis for determining size, the number of such enterprises by two major sectors, and the proportion of small TNC as a percentage of total enterprises. The share of small firms was particularly high in France and the UK. There was no common definition of what constitutes a small or medium size corporation. As can be seen from Table 4.2, not only different criteria, (assets, turnover, number of employees) were used, but the levels used in each category also differed. Only in the cases of UK and France was the same criteria, i.e. number of employees of 500 to categorize firms into large and small, has been used.

Table 4.2
The number of small TNCs, classified by country of origin,
size and sector

Country of origin	Size	Manufac- turing	Other sectors	Total	% of all TNCs
Canada	sales upto $18.4 mill.	80	515	595	58
France	20-499 employees	--	--	1600	80
Japan	upto 300 employees	238	103	341	23
UK	20-499 employees	--	--	1177	78
US	Assets upto $100 mill.	508	406	914	43

Source: UNCTC 1988. p.36.

Gullander (1976) in his study of determinants of entry into JV by firms in Europe also used employee numbers of 500 to describe firms into large and small. As this survey is concerned with UK based firms, using employee figures rather than other criteria was found preferable. Generally, number of employees for the latest year (1991) was taken to categorize firms into different sizes. The specific figure for the year was verified through comparing it to figures in other sources and also with figures of the past few years. Where there were significant variations averages were calculated. Therefore, firms with employee figures of 500 and above were classified as large, and those with employees less than 500 were classified as medium/small. Based on this criterion, the sample of 37 firms were: 19 large, and 18 medium/small.

Data analysis

Levels of measurement

Analytical techniques used in a survey research are determined by the levels of measurement, and the assumptions about the population distribution with regard to the specific sample survey. (Babbie, Robson 1985). There are four levels of measurement: nominal, ordinal, interval and ratio. Nuttall points out that while it is rare to meet ratio scales, and nominal scales are very common in social sciences, it is often difficult to distinguish between ordinal and interval scales. Treating attitudinal scales used in the social sciences as truly interval scaled has been controversial. (Weisberg & Bowen, Robson, Holmes, Nuttall 1986). The question often asked is, what would be the gravity of the risk of faulty conclusion in applying interval statistics on ordinal variables?

Nuttall argues that though many scales used in the social sciences may lack precisely equal intervals, they resemble interval scales more than ordinal scales. Though they feel uneasy about it, Weisberg and Bowen suggest that applying interval statistics on ordinal variables would not lead to faulty conclusions. (pp.195-96). Some statisticians, however, do not agree, (e.g. Stevens 1946, Holmes), who maintain that the use of such statistics as the mean, standard deviation or product moment correlation coefficient should apply only if the data are on interval or ratio scales. Holmes, for instance, points out that researchers using rating scales such as the semantic differential often calculate means regardless of the shape of a distribution. He asserts further that calculating mean scores for distributions which depart markedly from the normal or moderately skewed is neither desirable nor appropriate.

With regard to the survey study at hand, the values are expressed on a dimension of agreement/disagreement, important/not important with the posited statement, on a 5 point scale. The question whether the intervals were of equal size cannot be definitely ascertained. Further, the analysis carried out involved comparing and ranking variables. Therefore, the data analysis methods applied were those which were appropriate for the ordinal measurements.

Statistical tests

Tests of significance are of two types: parametric and non-parametric. Porkess (1988) describes the characteristics of these techniques as follows: Parametric tests of significance assume that the population distribution has a particular form (e.g. normal) and involve hypotheses about population parameters, i.e., mean, standard deviation, and covariance. Major parametric tests are t-test, product-moment correlation, and F-test. On the other hand, non-parametric tests of significance are those which make no assumptions concerning the parent population. All tests involving the ranks of data are non-parametric. Examples of such tests include Kendall's measure of concordance, Spearman's Rank correlation coefficient, the Mann-Whitney, the Friedman, the Kruskal-Wallis, etc.

As parametric tests are generally regarded to be stronger than non-parametric tests there is a temptation to use them even when the scales are not truly interval. To treat data as parametric, however, three conditions must be met: data must be at least interval scaled; scores should be normally distributed or nearly so; and there should be homogeneity of variance. (Weisberg & Bowen, Robson). Where these conditions are not met, then non-parametric statistics should be applied. (Siegel 1956, Steel & Torrie). As the characteristics of data in this study cannot be considered as truly interval, but are typically ordinal, the conditions for using parametric techniques are not sufficiently met. Therefore, the appropriate non-parametric tests are used to test the hypotheses.

Independent and related samples

In testing the hypothesis that a parameter in one population is equal to the parameter in another population, the appropriate test statistic depends on whether the samples are independent or related. When the measurement of the variable of interest in one sample in no way affects the measurement of the variable in another sample, the samples are independent. (Meddis, 1984). As outlined by Holmes, the most common conditions of independence between samples are a) when testing between mutually exclusive sub-groups in one sample, and b) when testing between independent samples drawn from the same population but usually at different points in time. On the other hand, when the measurement of the variable of interest in one sample can influence the measurement of the variables in an other sample, the samples are related. (Dillon et al., Robson).

With regard large and medium/small firm executives, the measurement of the variables in one group does in no way affect the measurement in the other group, and therefore, the two groups are independent samples. From a typology of statistical tests, (e.g. see Dillon et al. p.491) it can be noted that where the samples are two and independent, the level of measurement is ordinal, and the test is non-parametric, the appropriate test is the Mann-Whitney test. For the test of hypotheses with regard the appropriateness/importance of the various conditions, it is unlikely that the scores given by a respondent for alternative variables are independent. In other words the score given for an alternative is likely to be influenced by scores given to other alternatives.

Therefore, where the samples are three or more and related, the level of measurement is ordinal, and the test is non-parametric, the appropriate test is the Friedman test. The Friedman test and the Mann-Whitney test were used to test the hypotheses posited for analysis in Chapter 7.

Statistical package

A number of statistical computer packages can be used in marketing and management surveys, among them SPSS-X and MINITAB. Evans (1990) suggests that the former is often the choice for more substantial surveys. Among the softwares available to the researcher, the SPSS contained a large number of nonparametric tests with step by step guides of application. Moreover, the SPSS was available in PC version which allowed a convenient usage. Therefore, the SPSS/PC+ was used to analyze the survey data.

References

Artisien, P.F.(1985). *Joint Ventures in Yugoslav Industry*. Gower Publishing Co. Ltd.

Babbie, E.R.(1973). *Survey Research Methods*. Belmont: Wadsworth Publishing Co. Inc.

Barabba, V.P.(1990). 'The Marketing Research Encyclopedia', *Harvard Business Review*. January/February.

Bennett, R.(1986). 'Meaning and Method in Management Research', *Graduate Management Research*. Special Issue. Vol.3 No.3. pp.4-56.

Best of British: the Top 20,000 Companies, 1991. vol.1-5. Bristol: Jordan & Sons Ltd.

Britains Top Privately Owned Companies, 1991. Vol. 1-5. Bristol: Jordan and Sons Ltd.

Chernatony, L.de (1989). 'Achieving High Response Rates: a Survey of Postal Research', *Working Paper SWP9/89*. Cranfield: Cranfield School of Management.

_____, (1988). 'Getting the Most From Postal Research', *Working Paper SW23/88*. Cranfield: Cranfield School of Management.

Companies with British Interests in African countries 1990/91. London: the Department of Trade and Industry (DTI). (unpublished document).

Dillon, W.R. et al.(1990). *Marketing Research in a Marketing Environment*. 2nd edition. Boston: Richard D Irwin, Inc.

Dinham, B. & Hines, C.(1983). Agribusiness in Africa. London: Earth Resources Research Ltd.

Directory 1991-92. London: British Consultants Bureau.

Dooley, D.(1984). *Social Research Methods*. New Jersey: Prentice-Hall.

Edris, T.A. & Meidan, A.(1990). 'On the Reliability of Psychographic Research: Encouraging Signs for Measurement Accuracy and Methodology in Consumer Research', *European Journal of Marketing*. vol.24 no.3. pp.23-41.

European Food Trades Directory 1991-92. Vol.1. United Kingdom. 22nd Edition. London: Newman Books Ltd.

Evans, M.(1990). 'MINITAB: A Guide to Survey Data Entry and Analysis', *Graduate Management Research*. vol.4 no.4. Spring. pp. 36-61.

Exporter List 1991, Series 2. East Africa. Southport: Freight Information Services (FIS) Publications Ltd.

Exporter List 1991, Series 2. Nigeria and West Africa. Southport: Freight Information Services (FIS) Publications Ltd.

FAME (Financial Analysis Made Easy): Database of Accounts of Major Public & Private British Companies. Version 4.2. London: Jordans & Sons. 1992.

Fink, A. & Kosecoff, J.(1985). *How to Conduct Surveys: a Step-by-step Guide.* SAGE Publications.

Gatlung, J.(1969). *Theory and Methods of Social Research.* New York: Columbia University Press.

Gullander, S.(1976). 'Joint Ventures in Europe: Determinants of Entry', *International Studies of Management and Organizations.* Vol.6 no.1-2. Spring/Summer.

Holmes, C.(1974). 'A Statistical Evaluation of Rating Scales', *Journal of the Market Research Society.* Vol.16 no.2. pp.87-108.

Key British Enterprises 1992: Britain's Top 50,000 Companies. Vol. 1-6. High Wycombe: Dun & Bradstreet Ltd.

Kompass, United Kingdom 1991/92. Vol.II. Company Information. West Sussex: Reed Information Services Ltd.

Krausz, E. & Miller, S.H.(1974). *Social Research Design.* London: Longman Group Ltd.

'Leading European and UK Companies', *Financial Times.* January 13, 1992. (Separate Section pp.27-31).

Macleod, S. (ed) (1991). *The Directory of British Importers 1991. Vol. I & II.* Berkhamsted: Trade Research Publication.

Maya, R. & Tangoona, H.(1989). 'Ownership Structure of the Manufacturing Sector: vol. II', *Consultancy Reports No.9.* Harare: Zimbabwe Institute of Development Studies. (ZIDS).

Meddis, R.(1984). *Statistics Using Ranks: a Unified Approach.* Oxford: Basil Blackwell Publisher Ltd.

Miles, M.B. & Huberman, A.M.(1984). *Qualitative Data Analysis.* Beverly Hills: SAGE Publication Inc.

Miller, D.C.(1983). *Handbook of Research Design and Social Measurement.* 4th. ed. New York: Longman.

Norusis, M.J.(1988). *SPSS/PC+ V2.0 Base Manual.* Chicago: SPSS, Inc.

Nuttall D.L.(1986). *Block 5: Classification and Measurement.* Milton Keynes: Open University Press.

Oman, C.(1989). *New Forms of Investment in Developing Country Industries.* Paris: OECD.

Porkess, R.(1988). *Dictionary of Statistics.* Glasgow: Collins.

'Profit Margins Unchanged and Return on Capital Down', *The Grocer.* November 9, 1991. pp.34-6.

Robson, C.(1985). *Experiment, Design, and Statistics in Psychology.* 2nd edition. Harmondsworth: Penguin Books Ltd.

Siegel, S.(1956). *Nonparametric Tests for the Behavioural Sciences.* New York: McGraw-Hill book Company, Inc.

Smith, N.C.(1990). 'The Case Study: A Vital Yet Misunderstood Research Method for Management', *Graduate Management Research.* vol.4 no.4. pp.4-26.

Steel, G.D. & Torrie, J.H.(1980). *Principles and Procedures of Statistics: A Biometrical Approach.* 2nd. edition. Tokyo: McGraw-Hill Kogakusha, Ltd.

Stevens, S.S.(1946). 'On the Theory of Scales of Measurements. Science', vol. 103, pp. 677-80, in Nuttall D L (1986). *Block 5: Classification and Measurement.* Milton Keynes: Open University Press.

Sudman, S. (1983) 'Applied Sampling', in Rossi, P H et al. (eds). *Handbook of Survey Research.* Orlando: Academic Press Inc.

Tropical Growers Association (TGA): *Annual Report and Accounts 1989.* London 1990.

Tull, D.S. & Hawkins, D.I.(1984). *Marketing Research: Measurement and Method.* 3rd edition. Macmillan Publishing Company.

UNCTC (1988). *Transnational Corporations in World Development.* New York: United Nations.

UNCTC (1981). *Transnational Corporations in Food and Beverage Processing.* New York: United Nations.

Walizer, M.H. & Wienir, P.L.(1978). *Research Methods and Analysis: Searching for Relationships.* New York: Harper & Row.

Weisberg, H.F. & Brown, B.D.(1977). *An Introduction to Survey Research & Data Analysis.* San Fransisco: W H Freeman & Co.

Who Owns Whom 1991: United Kingdom and Republic of Ireland: vol. 1 & 2. High Wycombe: Dun & Bradstreet Ltd.

Yin, R.K.(1989). *Case Study Research: Design and Methods.* Applied social research methods series. vol.5. Newbury Park: SAGE Publications.

5 Exploring the experiences and opinions of UK executives: A pilot study

Introduction

The literature review has indicated that there exists a wide gap in understanding the determinants of joint venture (JV) formation in the agribusiness sector in sub-Saharan African countries (SSACs). Due to some different characteristics of agribusiness, and the general lack of previous study with regard to SSACs, a pilot study was found to be essential. Therefore, the major purpose of the pilot study was to verify the identified variables and to enhance the reliability of the research instruments: i.e., the case study protocol and the questionnaire, in the African and Agribusiness context.(1)

The specific objectives of the pilot study were, to find out:

i)   What were the most important international business participation modes or forms companies employed in SSACs;

ii)   How were a firm's objectives in its international business operations in SSACs commonly described;

iii)   How 'African countries' were understood by executives, and if there was a regional definition that can be more applicable to the situation;

iv)   Who were their host partners (current and prospective) and what were their opinions about them;

v)   How a 'joint venture' was understood by executives, and if there was a common understanding of the term;

vi)   How important were the ownership and management control issues in their decision to enter JVs in SSACs; and

vii) How do they evaluate the host country specific business environment, particularly the major barriers they experience in JV entry in SSACs.

Indepth personal interviews were conducted with senior executives of 10 UK based companies in the agribusiness sector regarding their opinions about and experiences in JVs in SSACs. An interview guide was used to streamline the discussion (Appendix E). The executives and the particular companies involved were selected because of their long experiences and association with agribusiness in Africa. 5 of the companies were large MNCs, and the remaining 5 were medium/small firms engaged in marketing, management and technical consultancy, and other related services. The interviews were conducted between June, 1990 and March, 1991; and the length of interview ranged between 1 hour and 2 hours. The chapter has 2 major sections; a) a summary of the opinions and experiences of the executives relevant to the study, and b) some conclusions and implications for the research design.

A summary of opinions and experiences of executives

Objectives and strategies

Generally, companies approached have got clearly defined objectives, and strategies to achieve these objectives in some cases defined by regions. For example, one large MNC, Company A(2), has a set out mission, objectives and strategy designed for Africa.

i)   *Africa vision statement:* a) in due course, some countries in Africa will take their place among the developed nations of the world; b) our vision is to establish Company A in this market and thereby to contribute to the economic growth of selected countries and the personal well being of their people; and c) we will achieve this primarily through improvement in agriculture and the processing businesses in which we are competent.

ii)   *Africa mission statement:* a) the mission of the Africa Division is to continue the development of a profitable physical presence in Africa which is complementary to Company A's ethics, goals and strategies; b) we will invest in asset based businesses in those countries and product lines which are conducive to long term growth and Company A's objectives; c) we will continue to seek trading and sourcing opportunities; d) we will recruit and train quality personnel; and e) our approach will be flexible to allow for different cultural, political and social customs in the different countries of Africa.

iii)   *Investment criteria:* Businesses in which we invest must satisfy the following 'musts': a) operate profitably: in this context profitability means a 5 year payback or less, based on cash low; b) allow us full management control; c) be able to be managed and staffed by us; and d) be able to be operated within Company A's code of ethics.

Business in which we invest should satisfy the following 'wants': a) allow the organization of the necessary raw materials; b) achieve a return on investment of 25% and a cash flow payback of 4 years; c) utilize the expertise, experience and technology possessed by Company A; d) allow the repatriation of profits and capital; e) be compatible with Company A's strategic profile; f)) allow us to play a role in the pricing decision process; g) be self sustaining on foreign exchange requirements; h) contribute to the development of critical mass; i) require an acceptable investment; j) be located in a workable financial environment; k) require a minimum amount of outside capital for investment; l) be located in countries with an infrastructure sufficient to support the business; m) allow us a majority ownership; n) enjoy a political environment of government support and non interference; o) have a government with economic policies favorable to our involvement; p) have a worthwhile market size and market share potential; q) have a sustainable competitive advantage; and r) have a market with a positive future trend and with growth potential.

Many company executives were found to be very cautious in committing investment in African countries; be it in the form of wholly owned subsidiaries (wos) or JVs. In the first place, irrespective of the region of operation, investment decisions in agribusiness are generally not easy to make because the production processes are relatively lengthy, exposure to natural calamities is common, and markets are generally unstable. This uncertainty could be compounded if the regional/country specific investment environment is not conducive. Executives stressed the profit and market expansion motives to be among the top priorities. They argued that they invest on behalf of the shareholders, and they want to be sure it is safe, brings satisfactory return, and this within a reasonable period of time. Some executives indicated that their policies on return on investment (ROI) and payback periods vary according to the political and economic stability and general conduciveness of the specific region. For example, one company maintains a policy of ROI of 25%, and a payback period of 4 years as a minimum condition for investing in an African country. These conditions are less stringent for other regions.

Further, companies generally tended to invest where they had previous presence in one form or another. It was also noted that companies envisage their involvement in African countries in a long term perspective. Therefore, they wanted to be sure that there was a good prospect, and ample room for expansion. Besides the home market in the host country, export opportunities to neighboring countries, existence of a capital market (stock exchange) were important considerations companies take into account in locating a JV in a particular country.

Types of host partners

Regarding preferences for host partners, the general inclination was towards the private firm. However, executives pointed out that such choice seldom reflects the reality, as availability of private firms as capable partners was the exception rather than the rule. A few have a company policy of not going into JVs where the potential host partner is a state owned firm. But the majority indicated that in most African countries state owned firms were the only capable partners endowed with ample resources, i.e. financial, manpower, organizational and various government support. Executives, therefore, have a policy of evaluating the opportunities case by case. Some mentioned cooperatives as possible alternatives in their choice of host partners.

Ownership and management control

In principle, there was a general appreciation by executives of the host governments' desire for local participation in the ownership of the ventures. For many of them, majority or 50% ownership by their company was considered desirable, but on the whole there appeared to be a willingness to be flexible.

One of the areas where executives seemed to hold unanimous opinion was with regard to management control. Executives insisted that inspite of the percentage in ownership, management should be their prerogative. This is because not only the success of the new enterprise, but their world-wide reputation would be at stake. Their managerial experience built over several decades, and often composed of individuals of multi-national and multi-cultural background would be the crucial factor in the success or failure of the venture. Besides, they argued, the new venture would have a better access to various services pooled at the foreign company's headquarters and strategic centers (e.g. research, technical and market innovations). Particularly when the product is for export to developed markets, where the competition is fierce and 'total quality management' has to be applied, managerial control should lie with the best equipped partner.

Commitment

While the primary concern appeared to be making profits and developing markets, there was also a strong tendency to identify their companies with the development programs of the host countries. They mentioned their role in the fulfillment of economic objectives; in the generation of employment, revenues (through taxes) and foreign exchange; in the development of natural resources, and in training manpower. Further, there appeared to be a tendency to commit resources in proportion to the level of equity ownership and management control.

The business environment

Barriers to investment in general and those particular to JVs generally tally to the literature. Executives' evaluation of political and economic situations varied; some indicating that they were 'used to it and can cope', while others felt that they have been a big barrier. Almost all interviewees mentioned repeated cases of indecisions, arbitrary and unilateral decisions by government officials and cases of corruption. Often the regulations were not so restrictive, but their implementation was inconsistent. In most cases there was lack of ethical business practice. They were of the opinion that such barriers as political and economic instability, market development, bureaucratic ways of decision making and inadequate infrastructure would take time to overcome.

Political and economic instabilities were expressed in terms of civil unrests, regional wars, frequent changes in government leadership, weak local currencies, inflation, recurrent foreign exchange crises, etc. Some indicated for the need of accurate information about JV opportunities. For instance, one executive responded 'where are the partners?..where is the project?..'.

The growing trend in privatization and general liberalization of policies in many African countries are followed with interest by company executives. Many interviewees expressed their hopes that privatization and other positive policies would be properly implemented. One expected outcome was that privatization would create new local partners, thereby enhancing the possibility of attracting foreign investors to form JVs. Generally, however, the optimism was tempered with caution. For instance, among the serious problems in privatization is a proper mechanism for determining realistic value of the company privatized; some executives mentioned their recent experiences where the estimations have been grossly overvalued. Many executives were also of the opinion that privatization by itself would mean little.

Summary and implications for the case and survey studies

Understanding a 'joint venture'

Almost all executives have got various experiences with JVs; most have been involved in one or a number of such responsibilities as feasibility studies, negotiating, operating, supervising, managing JVs in African countries and other DCs. Therefore, they were aware of the advantages, disadvantages and the problems of formation and operation of JVs. However, some considered licensing, agency and passive financial investments as JVs. Therefore, providing a precise definition of JV in the questionnaire was found essential.

Specifying a region of Africa

Though the executives had no difficulty in addressing the subject of JVs in the context of SSACs, most of their experiences and examples cited during the discussions were specific to a group of African countries with a common historical background. These countries were former British colonies, and presently they share common strong relations with the UK, and between themselves via the Commonwealth and other institutions. Therefore, it was noticed that the survey would attain better response rate and more relevant results if questions to executives in a questionnaire referred to this group of African countries, generally known as 'English-speaking African countries'. The countries are: Botswana, Gambia, Ghana, Kenya, Lesotho, Liberia, Malawi, Nigeria, Sierra Leone, Sudan, Swaziland, Tanzania, Uganda, Zambia and Zimbabwe.

Host partners

The literature on host partners generally distinguishes between privately owned firms, state-owned firms, public companies, and foreign firms in a host country. A clear preference is indicated for private sector firms as host partners. Executives appeared to show considerable flexibility as regards having state-owned firms as partners. Some executives indicated that they found in some countries pressure to deal with agricultural producers and marketing cooperatives in their search for partners for JVs. A new type of host partner, cooperatives, unique to agribusiness was identified for investigation in this study.

Lack of capable host partners have been emphasized by executives. Therefore identifying the strength and weaknesses of the various existing local enterprises, and how the major weaknesses can be overcome would be central issue for the case study.

Objectives and strategies

Though there have been indications that firms show a degree of commitment to host country interests, this however appears to be secondary. The primary objectives in international business were profits, market entry and penetration, sourcing and obtaining cost advantages through local resource utilization. JVs were regarded as important strategies to achieve these objectives.

Major barriers

Though small markets, lack of infrastructure, political and economic instabilities, were mentioned among the major constraints in the formation and expansion of JVs in African countries, 'poor policy implementation' and business ethics (bureaucracy, nepotism, bribery) have been stressed as the most serious obstacles. Executives welcomed incentives, but did not consider them as a critical factor that influence their decisions to form JVs.

In their evaluation of the host country specific entry determinants, executives have suggested that some factors were more serious than others. Establishing the relative importance of the factors that determine JV formation, and attempting to prioritize them for policy formulation and action in a bigger survey was therefore another major issue of interest for this study. The host country specific factors identified from the literature and verified through the pilot study added upto 23. These factors would form a part of the survey study. (see Appendix C).

Ownership and management control

Though the general tendency was towards majority ownership, executives appeared to show considerable flexibility as regards the percentage of ownership in JVs, but insisted on management control.

International business involvement modes

From the literature review, we can see that some authors limit the business involvement modes to a few, wholly owned affiliates, JVs and licensing (e.g. Davidson 1982), or go-it-alone, JVs, acquisitions/mergers (e.g. Gullander 1976), and still others to several (e.g. Cavusgil and Gauri 1990). A review of the various involvement modes along the comments of executives resulted with the following:

i)   From the literature, direct investment comprises of two major components: wos, and JVs. The executives have indicated that their decisions would vary significantly depending on the level of share and control the firm can achieve in a JV. The difference between the types of JVs was found to be an important area of enquiry, and therefore, majority JVs, minority JVs, and coownership (50-50) were identified as separate variables.

ii)   Management agreements were redefined as 'management and technical agreements' as the interviewees suggested that technical and management skills acquisitions go hand in hand.

iii)   Freidmann and Kalmanoff (1961) and many others assert the importance of import/export relations by indicating that JVs may develop from import/export activities. Executives interviewed in this pilot study have confirmed that import/export relations were the testing ground for more closer collaboration between them and their counterparts in the African countries. Therefore, import/export is maintained in the list of the important business involvement modes for the survey study.

iv)   Findings suggest that countertrade is more of a settlement of a business operation mainly involving export and imports, and therefore, it was not considered as a major variable in the acquisition of capital, technology and skills. Therefore, its characteristics are assumed to be encompassed in the export/import variable.

The core business involvement forms in the agribusiness sector in SSACs, and therefore the variables to be measured in the survey are a) wos, b) (foreign) majority JVs, c) coownership, d) (foreign) minority JVs, e) licensing, f) management/technical agreements, and g) import/export.

Notes

1   An earlier version of this pilot study is published as 'factors determining JV formation in the agribusiness sector of SSACs'. (see Selassie and Hill 1993).

2   Company A is a code given to one of the companies surveyed. The company is among the largest privately owned corporations in the world.

References

Cavusgil, S.T. & Ghauri, P.N.(1990). *Doing Business in Developing Countries: Entry and Negotiation Strategies.* London: Routldege.

Davidson, W.H.(1982). *Global Strategic Management.* New York: John Wiley and Sons.

Freidmann, W.G. & Kalmanoff, G.(1961). *Joint International Business Ventures.* New York: Columbia University Press.

Gullander, S.(1976). 'Joint Ventures in Europe: Determinants of Entry', *International Studies of Management and Organizations.* vol.1-2 no.6. Spring-Summer. pp.85-111.

Selassie, H.G. & Hill, R.W.(1993). 'Factors Determining Joint Venture Formation in the Agribusiness Sector in SSACs', *Journal of International Food and Agribusiness Marketing.* vol.5 no.1. pp.73-93.

6 The JV formation environment in a SSAC: A case study of Zimbabwe

Introduction

Among the three major determinants of joint venture (JV) formation in developing countries (DCs) discussed in the literature review are the home-country specific factors. The main components of the home-country specific factors are government policy, host partners, the home-country market, the foreign exchange situation, incentives and infrastructure. While these factors are also important in any type of foreign investment and trade, government policy and availability of capable partners have more impact on formation of JVs. It has been previously explained that these factors in particular and the business environment in general with regard to sub-Saharan African countries (SSACs) is better tackled through a case study approach than through other methods. (see Chapter 3). Accordingly, a case study of Zimbabwe has been undertaken.

During field work in Zimbabwe in the period August to October 1991, a number of companies, and other national and international organizations that are in one way or other involved in JV formation and promotion were identified and interviewed. In total, 32 organizations were contacted for gathering data; of these organizations 6 were JVs, 5 private and public companies, 5 parastatals, and 16 others (government departments, associations, international organizations, trade missions, etc.). Face-to-face interviews based on the case study protocol were conducted with executives of 16 of these organizations. Other 16 organizations were visited with the purpose of obtaining information of a general nature such as printed materials, comments on organizations of interest, and the general business environment.

In addition to the interviews, a mail questionnaire was sent out to assess the attitudes of small businesses towards joint venturing. The purpose was to identify food and agribusiness firms in the small business sector, and their particular needs in JV formation. 50 small businesses were selected at random from the files of the Indigenous Business Development Center (IBDC) (1) for the survey. 46 questionnaires were mailed to the managers of such enterprises, and 21 were filled in and returned, giving a response rate of 46%. The case study protocol which is used during the interview, and from which the questionnaire for the survey of indigenous entrepreneurs was extracted is given as Appendix B.

The case study report is presented in 7 sections. Section 1 is introduction. Section 2 outlines the objectives of the case study. In section 3 the research question and theoretical propositions generated for the case study are discussed. Section 4 describes the investment environment that influences JV formation in Zimbabwe. The results of the interviews with executives of the various companies and organizations are summarized in section 5. Finally, section 6 reports the summary and conclusions of the case study.

Objectives

i)   To explore the entry environment for foreign firms to form JVs in the food and agribusiness sector in Zimbabwe, particularly in terms of government policy, and availability of capable host partners,

ii)   To identify some areas for JV opportunities as suggested by executives in the food and agribusiness sector in Zimbabwe, and

iii)   To identify major barriers that inhibit JV formation in the food and agribusiness sector of Zimbabwe.

The research question

The research question for the case study is: how conducive is the JV entry environment for foreign firms in the food and agribusiness sector of Zimbabwe? If conducive, what are the strengths? If not conducive, what are the major barriers, and how can they be overcome?

The question deals with two major factors:

i)   Government policy: Does the Zimbabwe government promote JVs in the agribusiness sector of the economy, and if so, how effective has it been in attracting foreign partners?

ii)   Availability of capable host partners: Who are the potential host partners; what are their strengths and weaknesses, do they opt for JVs, and why?

Theoretical propositions

The following theoretical propositions were generated in order to analysis the data, match the various evidences, and arrive at conclusions. The propositions are based on the discussions given in Chapter 2, particularly the section dealing with why governments of DCs favor JVs. The propositions are stated as follows:

i) *Government policy*: Lacking many critical resources for their development programs, SSACs depend on external sources to acquire these resources. As a balancing mechanism in meeting the objectives of acquiring these resources and control over their economies they find joint venturing an attractive option. It is proposed that, therefore, these objectives are expressed as policies, and that strategies to promote JVs in terms of incentives and other supports are made available to JVs and/or to the partners. JVs established have benefited from such incentives and supports, and companies are expecting these benefits.

ii) *Host partners*: One of the major determinants of JV formation in DCs is the availability of capable partners in the host country. Host partners have different existing or potential strengths and weaknesses in resource allocation depending on their nature of organization and ownership structure. It is expected that local firms with ample resources are scarce and there is a need to promote the less capable ones with various supports.

Prospective host firms will look for foreign partners rather than Zimbabwean firms as partners. This is mainly for two reasons: a) the resources they seek from partners are not available within Zimbabwe, b) they aspire to inter the export market which is better accessed through foreign firms.

JV formation in DCs is generally preceded by other looser modes of business relations between the host firm and the foreign firm, such as import/export, agency, contract agreements, purchase/sales agreements, etc.

It is proposed that partners of JVs already set up had such looser business relationships and present local firms in import/export, agency, etc. aspire for turning their relations into JVs. It is expected that JVs operating have resulted from previous involvements of the partners in business relations, and host companies aspiring for JVs have got business relations with the prospective foreign firm(s).

Procedure and validity

The reasons for using the case study strategy, the case study design, and the importance of the case study protocol for enhancing the reliability of the case study are discussed in Chapter 4 of the book. The problem of validation of findings of qualitative research has been a major concern of social scientists. Miles and Huberman (1984) point out that qualitative researchers often emphasized the 'what' (the findings, the descriptions) and less on the 'how' (how one got the 'what'). They stress that validity can be enhanced by the adoption of step by step procedures in data collection and double-checking of findings, coupled with using multiple sources and modes of evidence. In this section, a description of how the case study was conducted, i.e, the procedure, and how this enhances the validity of the findings are discussed.

Procedure: Using the case study questions as a guide, the major portion of data is gathered through face to face interviews. The interviews were conducted in a form of open discussion, rather than seeking specific answers to specific questions, one by one. The discussion started with the researcher explaining the purpose of his visit, and asking the interviewee to share his views on the subject from his personal and his organization's experiences.

For example, the interviewee is asked to discuss the expected resource contribution of the prospective foreign partner for a new JV. The respondent explains in his own style, and the major points are duly noted by the researcher. Then he would be asked to identify the most important ones, if possible to rank them in their importance. From the response, the researcher notes the corresponding rank number for each resource item identified. Similarly, if for example, the respondent is an executive of a JV, he is asked what incentives were available to his venture at the beginning. If his reply indicates some incentives they are noted, and if he is sceptical and cannot mention any he will be asked if his reply is to mean no incentives. If this receives a consent then the code 'no' is noted along the appropriate item.

Other available information from published and unpublished sources are also referred to, in the mean time checking and comparing for clarity. When some interview items are vague or contradictory, clarification is sought by telephone or a second short interview. In most cases, there was no problem in following this procedure.

From the data thus gathered summary matrices were prepared. To make comparisons possible:

i)   Like organizations were grouped together. These are a) operating JVs, b) medium/small agribusiness firms forming JVs, c) large agribusiness firms seeking JVs, d) investment promotion organizations, e) foreign trade missions and f) small businesses.

ii)   Responses which were in phrases were transformed into standard codes. The codes were developed during the primary analysis in the field. Keys to codes and abbreviations are given with each matrix. The respondents were pressed to clarify each issue so that there will be no problem in coding the responses.

From the data presented in the matrices, comparisons are made, similarities and differences noted; and the pattern explained based on the propositions prepared before the field study.

Validity: To enhance validity of findings, the following have been undertaken:

i)   Theoretical propositions have been prepared.

ii)   To ensure representativeness the studied firms and organizations include various types, differentiated by business experience in joint venturing, and size (large and medium/small).

iii) Data were gathered from different sources: a) published and unpublished sources; and   b) from organizations of differing interests on the same issues: government institutions, executives of business firms, parents of JVs, JV managers, where possible different executives of the same organization, trade missions of major investor countries.

100

iv)   It is recommended in the methodologies literature that, besides using multiple sources of evidence, establishing a chain of evidence enhances validity. The fact that some firms are in various stages of the JV process has made possible to building a chain of evidence: operating JVs can indicate 'what has been' the condition for starting JVs, firms in the process of forming JVs indicate 'what is' the current condition, and those firms intending joint venturing 'what ought' be the condition for joint venturing.

The business environment affecting JV formation

A brief introduction to the economy

Zimbabwe is situated in south central Africa, and has a population of 8.64 million (1987). With an annual growth rate of 2.8%, the population is expected to reach 11.9 million by the year 2000. A UNIDO report(1990) describes Zimbabwe as a country with a well-developed manufacturing sector, prosperous commercial farming, varied mineral resources and a relatively dense infrastructure. It has a per capita income of Z$980 (1986 prices) (2), and is one of the few SSACs ranked among the middle-income countries.

In 1986 the manufacturing sector was the major contributor to the GDP, accounting for about 30% of the total (Table 6.1); with agriculture and mining contributing approximately 11% and 7% respectively. Agro-based products and minerals provide for 70% of the country's total exports.

Ownership structure in the manufacturing and farming sector

An important characteristic of the Zimbabwe economy is the significant position of foreign ownership. A study of the ownership structure of the manufacturing sector undertaken recently (Maya & Tongoona, 1989) surveyed 667 companies. Its findings indicated that of the total issued share capital of these companies, about 38% was foreign owned and 58% was locally owned. (3). Of the total local ownership the share of the government was about 15%. It can also be noted that agribusiness in general and the food processing industry in particular has a notably significant foreign capital share. For instance, in 1989 'foodstuffs' accounted for 36% of the total investment, with 47% of it being foreign and the rest local.

Table 6.1
Industrial origin of GDP, Zimbabwe (1981 and 1986) shown
in percentages

	1981 Percentage share	1986 Percentage share
Agriculture & forestry	15.9	11.4
Mining & quarrying	6.2	6.9
Manufacturing	25.1	30.2
Construction	3.4	2.9
Electricity & water	1.9	5.6
Transport & communication	7.5	5.7
Distribution, hotels, etc.	14.9	13.0
Finance & real estate	5.9	5.5
Public administration & defence	7.6	6.2
Services & other	11.5	12.6
Total GDP	100.0	100.0

Source: UNIDO, Zimbabwe: Investment Guide.

The foreign investment in the food processing industry has been made by a small number of MNCs with broad and diversified activities.(Batezat et al. 1986). The dominant ones are: Anglo-American and Lonrho in the grain industry; Rothmans, Lonrho and Dalgety in the production, processing and distribution of food products; Unilever and Nestle in the manufacture of edible oil and milk based food products; Lyons Brooke-Bond and Liebigs in the processing and canning of meat, fruits and vegetables; and Heinz and Dalgety in the processing and canning of vegetable based products.

The foreign investment came from companies in 14 different countries; Britain and South Africa being the dominant ones representing 54% and 17% respectively. Of the total foreign owned share capital 55% was 100% owned, 37% was in 51%-74% foreign owned category, and the remaining 8% in the 75%-99% category. Thus, the 'wholly owned subsidiaries' (wos) or the 100% category was the dominant form of foreign ownership.

It can be noticed that since foreign ownership is defined as to mean where foreign ownership accounts for 51% and above, foreign capital employed in the locally owned companies are not included. Therefore, the extent of foreign capital in the manufacturing sector could be much higher than indicated in the study.

The farming sector is composed of four sub-sectors:

i)   Large-scale commercial farming: consisting 4,500 farmers, owning 11.2 million hectares, and with about 20,000 tractors;

ii)   Small-scale commercial farming: consisting 8,600 farmers, owning 1.4 million hectares, and with 4,500 tractors;

iii)   Communal farming: consisting 850,000 households, owning 16.3 million hectares; and

iv)   Resettlement schemes: an arrangement for settling displaced persons, involving about an area of 3 million hectares.

Most agro-industries depend on the production of the first two sub-sectors, mainly on large-scale commercial farms. However, as the large scale farms are mostly owned by white Zimbabweans, there has been resentment by black Zimbabweans. There has been a great pressure for change, and it appears there will be a change sooner or later towards a more equitable redistribution of prime land. There is also uncertainty, particularly the impact of land reform on the agricultural production and the economy of the country, and opinions have been diverse and controversial.

Government objectives and policy

Since independence (1980), the government of Zimbabwe had as one of its objectives to reduce the foreign domination of the economy. Thus, "..the maximization of local ownership of industry in order to reduce the disbenefits associated with preponderant foreign control of economic activity in the country.." was reported to be as one of the objectives of the Ministry of Industry and Technology(Maya p. i). Another related objective outlined was effecting a transition in the ownership structure towards a socialist structure; implying a desire for heavy state involvement in investment. 'State capitalism' was to be welcomed as a necessary transitory stage to a socialist ownership structure.

The localization policy applied during the late 1980s can be expected to have substantially influenced the ownership ratios discussed previously. Though details are not available, there is evidence indicating that there has been a shift of ownership from foreign to local, particularly augmenting the government's share. Table 6.2 shows major share transfers that took place during 1987 and 1988. It emerges from the table that in all the 9 companies the transfer of shares are such that they have changed from being 'foreign companies' to being 'local companies'. Further, in 4 of the companies (Mardon Printers, Astra Corporation Ltd., Delta Corporation Ltd, and Hunyani Holdings), the government or its nominees obtained controlling shares in the localization process.

Since early 1991, the government has launched the 'Economic Structural Adjustment Program' (ESAP) to be implemented in a 5-years period (1991-1995) (4). The major elements of the program related to JV promotion and formation include: a) setting up of the Zimbabwe Investment Center (ZIC): a 'one-stop' investment approval body; b) simplification and liberalization of exchange controls on dividends & profit remittance; c) introduction and expansion of OGIL (Open General Import License) (5); d) price de-control; e) reduction of company basic tax rate; and f) rationalization of public enterprises (some to be sold in whole or in part, some to be reformed in to JVs with foreign and/or domestic private investors).

ESAP is generally welcomed by the business community in the country; and also has drawn support from the major developed countries, the World Bank, the IMF, and the African Development Bank. The Paris Donor's Consultation Meeting has pledged US$700 million for the first year of the Program; 20% of which is grant and the rest concessionary loan (6). But, the ESAP has also its critics, mainly from the academic circles and some sector of the political establishment.(e.g. see Moyo 1991, Mashakada 1991). The arguments include: the Program will aggravate the unemployment problem, it will worsen the social injustice (price de-control on essential products), the economy will be export oriented neglecting the broad social development objectives, and the Program is foreign imposed (the World Bank), etc.

Table 6.2
Transfer of shares in some companies (1987/88)

Company name	Former shareholders	(%)	Current Shareholders	(%)
Mardon Printers	Mardons(UK)	52	Zimbabwe News	100
	Zim. Newsp	35		
	Lever Br.(UK)	13		
Astra Corp. Ltd	Bommenede(SA)	100	Bommenede	14
			Zim.Gov't	80
			Workers' Trust	6
Kenning Motors	Kennings (UK)	100	Kennings(UK)	15
			Workers' Trust	30
			Local investors	55
Delta Corp Ltd.	SA Breweries	60	SA Breweries	29
	Local inv'rs	40	Local inv'rs	34
			Zim. Government	37
Schweppes Ltd	Schweppes(UK)	72	Schweppes(UK)	49
	Local inv'rs	28	Local investors	51
Hunyani Hold'gs	Guthrie (UK)	18	Mass Media Trust	37
	Barlow R.(SA)	66	IDC	25
	Old Mutual	5	Old Mutual	10
			Mandizvidza	13
Mutare Board&P	BPB Indus(UK)	100	BPB Industries	40
			Baringa Ltd.	60
Flexible Pack.	Kohler(SA)	100	Rusike	N/A
			5 businessmen	N/A
Hubert Davies	Mindeco(SA)	100	Employees Trust	100

Source: compiled from Confederation of Zimbabwe Industries notes.

Organizations promoting JVs

While a large number of organizations and agencies have promotional activities to encourage both foreign and domestic investors, the following have the greatest impact on the promotion of JVs. (Kunjeku, 1991).

-Zimbabwe National Chamber of Commerce (ZNCC),
-Zimbabwe Investment Center (ZIC),
-Confederation of Zimbabwe Industries (CZI),
-Zimbabwe Development Bank (ZDB),
-Indigenous Business Development Center (IBDC),
-African Project Development Facility (APDF),
-UNIDO,
-Developed countries representatives: the CDC (Commonwealth Development Corporation), JODC (Japan Overseas Development Corporation), FMO (Netherlands Development Finance Company Ltd.), SWEDFUND (Swedish Fund for Industrial Cooperation with DCs), SBI (Belgian Corporation for International Development), DEG (German Investment and Development Bank), FINNFUND (Finnish Fund for Industrial Development Corporation Ltd.), IFU (Danish Industrialization Fund for DCs);
-Others (7).

Technological and market oriented problems

Zimbabwe has one of the largest and well integrated manufacturing sectors in sub-Saharan Africa. This is partly attributed to government policies of the UDI period. The sanctions imposed on the country by the international community during this period led the government to pursue a policy of self sufficiency in manufactured goods, emphasizing import substitution. During the late 1970s and the early post independence period, however, the manufacturing sector including the food processing industry suffered from obsolescence of machinery, replacement efforts being frustrated by shortages of foreign currency.(Batezat p.30). This has affected particularly the export oriented food manufacturing sector (e.g. meat, fruits and vegetables processing). Further, a three year widespread drought (1981-84) and the international recession (1982-83) which affected production and foreign exchange receipts from exports have aggravated the situation.

Therefore some firms, to overcome the shortcomings in technology and capital, have resorted to seeking cooperation with foreign investors. This has not been easy, however. The domestic markets for most processed products are rather small. Some processed products constituted a 'luxury' to the majority of the population in the domestic market, and exporting faced stiff competition and protectionism.

A summary report of interview results

This section presents the opinions and attitudes of interviewed executives and officials of various organizations on the basis of questions in the case study protocol. They are grouped into 6, namely: operating JVs, medium/small firms in the process of forming JV, large firms seeking JV partners, organizations promoting investment including JV, trade missions to Zimbabwe, and small businesses.

Operating JVs

i) Olivine: Olivine is a JV formed between H.J.Heinz Company (51%), and the Government of Zimbabwe (49%). The major products of the firm are cooking oil, margarine, soaps, canned foods, bakers' fats, protein meals, and candles. Olivine is widely regarded as a successful JV and no major problem has been reported to exist between the partners. The only problem mentioned was government control on prices of some inputs and finished products.

An important factor to the success appears to originate from the predecessor of the JV being a well established firm with prominent market position for 50 years. This has contributed to the high commitment of Heinz, and also to the subsequent success of the JV company. The major contributions of Heinz were improved technology (renovation of machinery), technical know how and new products development.

The harmony in the relation of the partners is an indication of the fact that both have achieved their respective objectives. The JV has enabled Heinz achieve its corporate strategy of expansion, getting a critical mass in Zimbabwe (and southern Africa) through acquisition rather than green field venturing; it also has a majority share-holding. The satisfaction of the government comes from employment, revenue from taxes, foreign exchange through the exports, innovations in agricultural production and product development, and human resource development through the training scheme. Probably as important is the role Olivine plays as an example to show how a successful JV can be formed in partnership with the government.

A process of change in the management style can be noted from the various interviews and a review of the different issues of the quarterly journal (Olivine Today, 1991/90) of the company. The company has slowly moved from a family style of management to corporate management style. Directors, department heads and other positions are increasingly filled by qualified professionals with wide experiences. An elaborate training scheme for personnel at all levels is provided and job descriptions and other management tools are being implemented.

Parallel to this has been a shift in the management orientation of the company. In the earlier years (up to 1985) management was concerned with boosting production, as whatever the firm produced had a ready market. The next 3 to 4 years the emphasis was on rationalization of costs and there have been various managerial steps taken to minimize operating costs. The last 2 years have been marked by a shift to marketing with a separate Marketing Department being created and a Marketing Manager appointed. The main objective of the firm is now orientated towards 'satisfying the customer', and 'improving the firm's competitive position'; TQM (total quality management) has been introduced and widely implemented, and more has been spent on advertizing. A review of the distribution channels and the product mix, and a plan to recruit brand managers, are among the tasks being currently undertaken by the Marketing Department. Thus, a clear trend can be noticed in management orientation: from production, then to finance and finally to marketing.

ii) Rusitu Valley Development Company (RVDC): The RVDC is a 50-50 JV formed between the Commonwealth Development Corporation (CDC) and the Agricultural Development Authority (ADA). CDC's participation in the JV is a component of British Government assistance to Zimbabwe. The ADA contributed in local finance, land and other farm infrastructure while the CDC's contributions constituted of machinery, management and other inputs requiring foreign exchange.

RVDC seems to be a less successful JV as it appears that there are misunderstandings between the partners. The ADA are not satisfied by the way the company is managed, which apparently, is the responsibility of the CDC. As the RVDC has been running at a loss since its inception (ADA, 1991), it is not clear whether it was established for 'development' objectives, and not as such to be profitable.

On the other hand, the CDC blame the host partners for failing in their commitments. Besides their general disinterest, the host partners backed away from presenting and pushing proposals to the government for the improvement of milk prices. The low milk price, which is regulated by government is the basis of the financial crisis the JV faced. Among the options being considered to bring improvement for the future is through other JVs.(CDC, 1991). Suggested JVs include a) between RVDC and Nestle, (the Milk Marketing Board might be included); and b) between RVDC and Tanganda for developing a 500 ha. of tea. Some of these evidences support the instability of 50-50 JVs highlighted in the JV literature. In 50-50 JVs their is often less commitment and disagreements on the partners respective responsibilities.

iii)Chipiwa Settlement Scheme (CSS): The CSS was undertaken as a JV cooperation between Anglo-American Corporation and the Government of Zimbabwe. Anglo-American Corporation provided the necessary machinery, management and technical know-how required for cane production, while the government provided the land, finance (mainly in long term lone to the settlers), and social experts and workers to organize the settlement program. Over the last 10 years, a large scale land development, agricultural production and settlement of about 191 people have taken place (9). This settlement scheme is a unique case where the major elements of 'sustainable development' have been successfully applied. Sustainable development in the agricultural and rural sectors in DCs would imply, as outlined by FAO (IAD, 1991), the following: a) first and foremost, meeting the basic nutritional requirements of present and future generations; b) providing durable employment, sufficient incomes and decent working and living conditions for rural people; and c) reducing the vulnerability of the agricultural sector to adverse natural and socio-economic factors and other risks, and strengthen self-reliance.

The project has, by and large, achieved most of the criteria outlined above through providing employment, generating sufficient incomes, and production of food as well as cash crops by applying advanced technical methods, thereby strengthening self-reliance. Since it is a short term project, and since the partners are not expecting a joint profit, CSS may not qualify as a JV seen in view of the definition adopted for this study. However, it is an interesting partnership which can serve as a model where governments and large agribusiness companies can cooperate to bring about development to rural areas.

i) Oceanic Fruits: This company is engaged in the export of horticultural products to Europe. Though the company produces some of the products, most of the export is acquired from other producers on consignment basis. The foreign company markets the products and pays the proceeds after deducting expenses and margins. Though this is basically an agency relationship, the manager of the company considers his relation with the foreign company as that of a JV because "they share the same objectives, the commitment and trust between them is high, and they share on the risk". The relation is expected to grow in the near future as the investment is going to grow and formal shareholding will be effected.

The objective of the Oceanic in a JV is to diversify, from just production to processing and packaging, and also increase the types of the fruits and vegetables. The present arrangement has helped to step into foreign markets, to get technical support (in quality control, packaging and transportation) but only in a small way. In the JV the foreign partner is expected to provide the necessary machinery and equipment for processing and market guarantee for the export part of the sales. Oceanic can take responsibility of supplying the raw materials (from own farms and contracting from other growers), and local finance, and management. So far the management indicated that they are not aware of any support or incentive available to them. The share in the JV is negotiable, but they favor the 50-50 option if possible.

ii) African Produce Marketing Pvt. Ltd. (APM): APM is a family business employing 3 persons, and mainly engaged in trading and food distribution. Recently, it has diversified into marketing consultancy and export. APM has many project ideas in processing and marketing of horticultural and food products but finds itself lacking in finance and technological skills.

The company has been seeking foreign partners that can contribute the resources the company lacks: finance, machinery and access to foreign markets. They count on the managerial skill of the executive manager which can be better utilized, thorough knowledge of the internal and regional markets; and some investible projects studied by the company. APM is currently considering two JV partnerships with two foreign firms, one Swiss and the other UK based. The company had known the prospective partners for a long time and they have undertaken some joint business operations on project basis. Their experience has shown that foreign investors would like the prospective host partner to be in a strong position, and be able to contribute substantial resources (financial as well as material -buildings, equipment, transport facilities, etc.).

They are generally dissatisfied with the support available to small companies. The project approval process has also not been encouraging. They expect share in the JV would be in proportion to contributions, and they are ready to take minority position if that will be the case.

All companies in this group have shown more flexibility as regards the level of share ownership desired and the organizational form of the JV. Support from national and international organizations are not generally available. It appears seeking for interested partners is a sole affair of the management of the particular firms which some find to be difficult. From these cases, the need for intermediaries that can assist medium/small firms to become more capable partners is apparent.

iii) Cold Comfort Farm Trust (CCFT): The CCFT is a local non-profit making organization engaged in promoting social and economic development in the rural regions. It is mainly involved in agricultural production, marketing and extension; promoting cooperatives, and training. It seeks for partners to expand along present lines, to diversify and to enter export markets. The CCFT was pleased with the results of the 'JV cooperation' with Feder Coop of Ravenna, Italy during 1990 (CCFT, 1991). Ravenna provided some seedlings which CCFT used to produce strawberries on experimental basis and sold the harvest to hotels in Harare. A formal JV between the CCFT and another Italian company is in the process of formation for production and export of strawberries. Though other JVs (in sericulture, food processing and canning) are also under consideration, all the projects are at their early stages. The foreign partners are expected to provide financial and technical know-how, and market access. The CCFT initiates and participates directly at the beginning, but step by step hands over to the cooperatives which are to replace it and become the sole host partners. The agricultural land it controls and those belonging to the cooperatives, the manpower attached to these lands, some volunteer experts the CCFT manages to recruit from mainly the developed countries are the main resources they have as contributions.

The CCFT's catalytic role to improve the cooperatives is a very important element; such as the bringing together of the coop. products for marketing domestically, as well as for export, which the cooperatives individually could not manage. Further, each cooperative would be too weak and too remote for any prospective foreign partner to show interest in its business. As a non-profit making organization CCFT gets some material

111

and financial support from private and international organizations. However, they find the project approval process very slow.

Large firms seeking JV partners

i) Cairns Holdings Ltd. Cairns Holdings Ltd. is a large public company established in Zimbabwe more than 60 years ago. It undertakes diversified business activities, the major of which is agro-processing (foodstuffs and beverages). Its annual turnover is about Z$ 150 million, and employees about 1,200 people. The company's operations are spread in the different regions of the country and other neighboring countries.

The company is actively seeking for JVs with foreign companies, because 'JVs are the quickest way to catch up with latest technology', as the Technical Director of the company put it. Currently, they are negotiating JVs with Danish and Belgian companies respectively for their coffee and fish processing operations. Their objective in JVs is to acquire latest technology in food processing, renovation of old machinery, and get access to foreign markets. On their part, they have strong basis in factory infrastructure, trained manpower, local finance and internal and regional market network. Due to their long experience in the food industry, they feel they are in a position to produce high quality agricultural products for processing and exporting to markets of the developed economies. They indicated that they get some locational and tax concessions, which apply generally. While share ownership is the outcome of the negotiation process, they favor owning the majority stake. Organizationally, either forming separate ventures or improving the present installations are possible. For example, in the case of coffee processing, the requirement is replacing a section of the existing factory (requiring about Z$ 10 million in foreign currency) while the fish project is a new start up.

Since they have got long time associations with a number of MNCs, they have no problem in seeking for prospective partners. On the whole, they are satisfied with the progress they are making towards forming the JVs.

ii) Hunyani Holdings Ltd.: Hunyani Holdings Ltd. is a public company with major operations in paper manufacturing and packaging. Its business activities include forestry development, timber milling., paper and paper products, folding cartoons, labels, corrugated containers for various products including foodstuff and beverages, tobacco, cattle and pig production. The company's operations are distributed throughout the country with about 12 subsidiaries, annual turnover of Z$165 million, and with a work force of about 2,900.

Hunyani Agri-forestry Ltd., one of its subsidiaries, has got a program of expanding it livestock operations, and diversifying in to meat processing, producing and processing horticultural products. A partner in a JV is sought to take up these operations and also to be able to enter foreign (European) markets. At present they are at project formulation stage as a basis for negotiating with prospective partners. They recognize their access to agri-land, considerable managerial capabilities, infrastructural, and financial resources as the strength the prospective partner would count on. Their most pressing needs in a JV are technical know-how, new product ideas, export market access and supply of advanced technology. Level of ownership is negotiable but they consider 50-50 ownership is desired by them.

Investment promotion organizations

Among the organizations promoting foreign investment, including JVs listed previously, the most involved organizations are the ZIC, CZI, ZNCC, and ZDB. These organizations have been contacted and interviewed. The most positive attitude about government policy came from the ZIC. This may be because it is nearer to current government policy. Though they encourage JVs in general they, however, are not in a position to give any specific incentive or support to JVs. What ever incentive or support given, such as tax concessions, locational allowances are administered to all new ventures inspite of their organizational form. ZIC indicated that JVs generally enjoy other 'intangible advantages'; such as 'speedier approval of the venture'. While ZDB agrees, the other two are not sure of such an advantage. All the four organizations felt that considerable support is available from them to assist potential partners but CZI and ZNCC indicated that they lack resources to be more effective.

It appears that the resort to JVs by foreign firms could be as a second best, after failing to establish a wos. Sometimes, therefore, JVs could be more convenient to set up than wos which are still looked upon with some hostility.

Trade missions

To gather some opinions of foreign interests trade missions of the UK, the US, Japan and Germany were visited. Their views were remarkably similar.

113

They agree that there is a general preference for JVs by the government and the local elite. Their general assessment of the business environment is not one of satisfaction. One representative mentioned the problem of 'trust'. He mentioned of a case where a JV agreement has been concluded between a company from his country and Zimbabwean interests. But within the same year, another JV agreement was signed with a European firm and Zimbabwean interests for producing the same type of product. As the market was not large enough the first firm had to withdraw from the JV agreement.

Another representative mentioned that 'the socialist rhetoric', the effectively 'one-party system' do not make investors welcome. They indicated the necessity of signing bilateral investment guarantees between Zimbabwean government and their respective governments.

The survey of small indigenous businesses

i) Business characteristics: Questionnaires were mailed to 46 small businesses which are members of the Indigenous Business Development Center (IBDC), and 21 were received appropriately completed, resulting in 46% response rate. The survey was conducted in September 1991. Of the respondents, all but two were private companies. The two did not clearly indicate the type of their enterprises.

Table 6.3
Length of business experiences

Period established	No. of respondents	(%)
1980 and before	1	5
1981 - 1985	4	19
1986 - 1988	2	10
Since 1989	12	57
No reply	2	10
Total	21	101[*]

[*]Total percentage is more than 100 because of rounding off.

The majority of the firms were quite young: 57% of them being established since 1989 (Table 6.3). Only one firm was in business during the independence of the country. Regarding the type of their business operations most firms, particularly those in the service sector mentioned different kinds.

Table 6.4 shows the operations undertaken, and the frequency of the particular operation mentioned by respondents, and the respective percentages.

Table 6.4
Types of business operations undertaken

Business types	No. of respondents	(%)
Manufacturing		
Steel based	2	11
Garment making	2	11
Electrical	2	11
Furniture	1	6
Cosmetics	1	6
Food processing	1	6
Services		
Transport & communication	3	17
Construction	2	11
Import/export	2	11
General trading services	9	50
Consultancy	1	6
Farming (commercial)	1	6
Mining	1	6

While most firms in the manufacturing sector have mentioned only one type of operation, the situation is not so with those in the service sector. Most have mentioned a range of activities as their business operations.

Taking only the basic operation of the firms, they can be grouped as follows: manufacturing 33%, services 56%, and others (farming and mining) 11%.

ii) *Attitudes towards JVs:* Asked if a JV partnership is desired by their companies, 18 (86%) responded yes, while only 3 (14%) said no. The 3 firms that did not desire a JV relationship felt that they can manage by themselves with the resources they have got. Of those who expressed a desire for a JV, respondents have given one or a combination of their reasons as shown in Table 6.5.

Table 6.5
Reasons for wanting a JV partnership

Reasons stated	No. of respondents	(%)
Access to export markets	7	41
Access to technology	4	24
Finance (including foreign exchange)	9	53
Machinery	5	29
Resources for expansion/ diversification	7	41
Others (supplies, high skills, & new ideas)	5	29
No reply	1	6

iii)*Resource allocations, organizational forms, and level of control anticipated:* The resources the respondents would be ready and able to contribute towards a JV are indicated in Table 6.6. Regarding the organizational form the JV is to take, most respondents (67%) foresee the 'improvement and expansion' of their existing firm, while some (22%) foresee establishing 'a new and separate' entity. 11% were not clear in their choice.(Table 6.7).

Table 6.6

Resources to be made available by small businesses for JVs

Types of resources	No. of respondents	(%)
Buildings	11	65
Land	8	47
Finance (cash)	9	53
Existing business facilities	10	59
Management & technical skills	4	24
Manpower	2	12
Other (rights to minerals)	1	6
Not clear	1	6

Table 6.7

Organizational forms envisaged by small businesses for their JVs

Organizational form	No. of respondents	(%)
A new & separate firm	4	22
Improve/expand existing firm	12	67
Either one of the above	2	11
Total	18	100

As regards the control of the JV, many prefer it to be the outcome of the negotiation (61%), some preferred majority share control (11%), and the rest (28%) would settle for a 50-50% share (Table 6.8).

Table 6.8
The level of control desired by small businesses in a JV

Control desired (percentage share)	No. of respondents	(%)
Equal share (50/50)	5	28
Majority (>50%)	2	11
Minority (<50%)	--	--
Negotiable	11	61
Total	18	100

No firm chose the minority position; which however, in reality is the most likely alternative. The fact that a substantial majority indicated to settle the issue in the negotiation would mean that the minority option in effect is still open.

iv) Search for partners and associated problems: Asked whether their prospective partner would be available within the country (Zimbabwe), 22% replied either 'yes', 67% 'no', and the remaining 11% were undecided. (Table 6.9). It can be inferred from this that the majority of the firms expect their partners to be foreign firms, leading to the formation of international JVs.

Table 6.9
Availability of the prospective partner within the country

Reply	No. of respondents	(%)
Yes	4	22
No	12	67
Undecided	2	11
Total	18	100

Asked to indicate common problems faced in the process of identifying a suitable partner, the responses were as shown in Table 6.10.

Table 6.10
Problems faced by small businesses in seeking for partners

Type of problem	No. of respondents	(%)
Companies showed little interest	3	17
Awaiting responses	3	17
Do not know how to go about looking		
Do not know how to go about looking for a partner	2	11
No specific problem mentioned	6	33
Did not reply	4	22
Total	18	100

Only 2 firms (11%) said they have received some kind of assistance in seeking for a partner, 78% did not get any assistance, and 11% did not respond to the question (Table 6.11). The only organization mentioned to have rendered any assistance is the IBDC.

Table 6.11
Assistance provided to small businesses

Any support	No. of respondents	(%)
Yes	2	11
No	14	78
No reply	2	11
Total	18	100

This section reveals that most small businesses belong to the services sector, and they are thin in the other sector, particularly in the food and agribusiness sector. This may be that small agribusinesses may be registered with other institutions as cooperatives and farmers associations. The survey, though may not help to generalize in the context of agribusiness, nevertheless contributes to explain the JV formation environment in the small business sector in general.

Summary and conclusion

Government policy

During the last decade Zimbabwean government policy towards the foreign investor has not been favorable: there has been pressure for indigenization, and profit and capital repatriation has been restricted. This led to a large scale divestment by foreign companies and very little inflow of new foreign investment. Though there has been substantial changes since 1990 which have eased the situation, foreign interests appear to be still wary bearing in mind their previous experiences.

The position of the government has not drawn favor with the foreign interests. International organizations, trade missions, banks and some foreign held companies are of the opinion that the government though appearing to support privatization, its involvement is on the rise, and policy formulated are often not clear, stable, nor properly implemented.

Though the Zimbabwean government has expressed guarantees that there will be no nationalization and expropriations, this is not found to be sufficient by many foreign interests. Separate bilateral agreements are required with the governments of countries which have the highest number of prospective investors (e.g. UK, USA and Germany) before such countries will fully commit themselves to encouraging investment by their companies.

No particular incentives or advantages provided for JVs are in evidence. All informants, established JVs, JVs under the process of formation, and even government organizations could not suggest any particular incentive or support provided. What ever incentive or support exist are common to all investors, and not based on the nature of the recipient organization.

The prediction that JVs or their partners enjoy special status, therefore, cannot be supported. It may be concluded that if incentives were important determinants of JV formation, then their absence have contributed to the slow growth of JV formation in the agribusiness sector in Zimbabwe. Yet, the government has expressed in its policy statements that Zimbabwean participation is highly desirable, implying that JV partnerships are preferred. If JVs are preferred, then support and incentives of material significance should be provided for the partners or the JV itself (e.g. full and timely repatriation of profits for the foreign partner, tax concessions, financial support to the host partner, allocation of foreign exchange, etc.).

Capabilities of potential host partners

Generally, almost all contacted companies and involved organizations have indicated strong interest and enthusiasm for JVs. As regards local companies, however, their potential as capable host partners varies substantially.

Many big corporations in agribusiness in Zimbabwe are of the opinion that they are financially strong and have got ample technical base to undertake agricultural production and processing by their own. However, almost all the interviewed executives indicated the need for JV partnerships with foreign companies in some particular circumstances. The need for JV partnership are felt in such situations as the following: a) acquiring up-to-date technology; b) undertaking new business activities which are out of the mainstream of the firm's activities; c) to overcome difficulties in obtaining foreign exchange permits to finance plants and machineries; and d) to enter markets of the developed economies.

The large local companies, with their large resources, experiences, marketing networks, and production bases, have wider opportunities to present themselves as capable partners to interested foreign investors. The same cannot be said about the medium/small companies. They generally lack the resources to attract and convince the prospective foreign investor to go into partnerships. The reluctance of the foreign firms to go into equity partnerships, for instance, with the African Produce Marketing Ltd., and with Oceanic Fruits can be explained in these terms.

From this study of various companies, a pattern has emerged which groups host partners into three: readily capable partners, potentially capable partners, and incapable partners.

i) Readily capable partners: can be described as those companies with substantial resources and those that can commit financial, technical and managerial resources. They are long established and have developed markets, channels of distributions, and a network of business relations. This group may not require any assistance in setting up JVs.

ii) Potentially capable partners: may be described as those companies which are medium or small in size, often with enthusiastic management, but short of resources to grow or to diversify. The situation of the second group calls for a 'fourth link' in JV formation, that plays the role of strengthening the position of the host partner on the one hand, and on the other, the confidence of the prospective foreign partner. Thus, a JV formation framewrok can be suggested that would be appropriate where there is a lack of readily capable host partners, but there are potentially capable host partners. This framework can be adopted to specific needs of prospective partners, countries and donor organizations.

Conceptually, the 4th link can be a non-profit seeking organization sponsored by the governments of the developed economies, donor international organizations and or private organizations. The basic assumption made in building the framwork is that such organizations are committed to playing a role in the development of African countries by providing various aid programs. This is nothing new, but there has been doubts as to the effectiveness of past aid programs, the major portion of which were administered through government institutions of the DC concerned.

Recently there was not only the need for more aid but a rethinking of how aid is implemented. Among the options gaining more support is the development of entrepreneurship and privatization. Among the basic steps that may be taken urgently is supporting the medium/small firms since they are widely spread in different regions of SSACs, and they can play significant role in the integration of the market.

The salient characteristics of the 4th link can be described as follows:

-Participates in the JV by contributing resources the host partner is unable to provide, particularly foreign currency;

-Provides guarantee for the acquisition of machinery and equipment, if the JV required importation of such machinery;

-Guarantees the profit repatriation of the foreign partner through its injection of foreign currency;

-Works along with chambers of commerce, and other trade associations which represent entrepreneurs and business and which generally are more committed and less bureaucratic;

-The fourth link may be temporary, until the JV gets maturity. Its share can be bought by the existing partners or by new partners.

iii)Incapable partners: refers to those companies which are much similar to the second group but relatively recent in their establishment, thus lacking in experience and specialization, and did not make any sustainable breakthrough in the home market. The immediate needs appear to be establishing themselves in the domestic markets, and various government assistances such as finding appropriate accommodation for their projects (including factory units), concessionary loans, training, market and management development are called for.

Attitudes towards JVs

The study indicated that there is a general enthusiasm for the JV mode from all concerned. The government finds JVs attractive. This has been expressed in its economic policy statement, by establishing promotional offices, and itself involving in JVs. Private and public firms contacted were actively looking for partners, usually with project proposals for implementation at hand. Small and medium firms appear even more enthusiastic, though most lack the necessary preconditions that make a capable host partner.

Some areas of JV opportunities

The major resources and attributes needed by local firms as contribution of the foreign partner are export market access, improved technology (in terms of technical know-how and machinery) and new product ideas. The major resources and attributes the host partners are capable of contributing towards a JV are: internal market network, existing factory/business facilities, finance (local currency) and raw material supplies. There are some evidences to suggest that larger firms are more able in the variety or extent of resources and attributes they can offer than medium/small firms. For instance, Hunyani and Cairns have management know-how and technical know-how in their list of possible contributions towards the JV.

The situations discussed above in this report indicate that joint venturing opportunities are strongly linked with the following:

-Renovation of (replacement of obsolete) machineries and equipment;

-Export oriented production which would meet stiff competition, and therefore, requiring high quality and efficient production and distribution system;

-Privatization of state owned companies;

-Expansion and integration of regional markets, and;

-Local medium/small entrepreneurs who aspire to satisfy niche markets.

Constraints for JV formation

Some of the major constraints mentioned by interviewees are summarized as follows.

Policies: policies do not specifically favor JVs, and are inconsistent in their application;

Market size: Zimbabwean market, though not small by African standard, is limited to support several competing agribusiness firms. For instance, Olivine with about 1500 employees is one of the largest firms in the sector, and enjoys 50% of the national market for edible oil. The other 50% is shared by a few other firms. Any growth in demand is taken up by existing firms, making entry for new firms difficult. The rise in income of the rural population and their absorption in the market system, and integration of the regional markets could create better opportunities.

Price control: Some prices on 'essential' products are regulated by the government. Investors do not find processing and marketing such products profitable or attractive. An example usually mentioned is milk. The Milk Marketing Board is in chronic financial difficulties. The problem faced by RVDC, one of the JVs covered in this study, is partly explained by the low prices it gets for milk.

Shortages of foreign exchange: This is by far among the severest problems both for local (for importing parts and machinery, raw materials), as well as foreign firms (capital and profit repatriation).

Skills and resources: Local firms find the response of foreign firms usually reluctant and discouraging. There are indications that most local firms lack the skill and other resources to prepare and propose investable projects to attract partners. Many firms, particularly in the medium/small category, do not know how to go about searching for a partner.

Distance: the location of Zimbabwe, in relation to some of the investor countries, e.g. Japan, USA, Europe make venturing too expensive for the foreign companies. This is of course not specific to Zimbabwe, it may be applicable to the other SSACs as well.

Others: Though difficult to verify in such a study bureaucratic delays and unethical practices in the approval process is repeatedly mentioned by medium/small firms and some foreign companies.

Some implications

To play a more effective role in the economy JVs have to be promoted through implementing clear and supportive policies. Given the general preference for wos by foreign firms, they have to be wooed into JVs. Discriminative tax incentives and profit repatriation could stimulate them more towards joint venturing. Information and promotion should be marketing oriented, putting forward the advantage the foreign investor could attain in a JV, and how government and other concerned bodies will handle the various problems and obstacles that the foreign firm may face.

Promoting JVs for exportable products, while a worthwhile effort, need be accompanies by strategies for motivating the domestic market for the same products. Given the stiff competition in the international market, firms need to expand in the home market, and sometimes use this solid basis while adjusting to market problems in the international market. In fact, for the JV, the home market and export market are complementary. Government policy and resources need be concentrated on raising the income level of the population, and bringing the rural population into the mainstream. However long term it may seem, it is a necessary condition for attracting foreign investment in a level that will have positive impact for development.

The reluctance of foreign firms to take state owned firms as partners on the one hand, and the general paucity of capable private firms on the other, calls for a strong program of support and promotion of the medium/small private firms. Such support can come from the national government, international organizations, and donor agencies. By making many host firms capable, foreign firms can have more choice and confidence in forming JVs.

Due to the shortage of foreign exchange that restrict repatriation of profit and capital, and the smallness of national markets, governments and local firms in SSACs may be tempted to look for partners from other DCs, particularly Asian countries. Within Africa, the changing situation in the Republic of South Africa, which has resources comparable to developed countries, can have an impact particularly to the southern African countries.

The resources made available by host partners in agribusiness lack uniqueness, placing them in a weaker position. Due to this, host partners are more likely to accept a minority position in a JV. In most cases, JVs grow from previous business relations between would be partners. While this is generally the case, where the host firm is a large organization with reputation and success records, foreign firms may be willing to go into JVs directly.

With regard to the organizational form of a JV, larger local firms tend to aspire for 'a new and separate venture', while medium/small ones look for 'improve/expand existing facilities'. This can be an additional constraint in the case of medium/small firms. Foreign firms may find it difficult to involve in an already established business. The local firm also may feel threatened by assumed or real possibility of a 'take-over' by the incoming partner.

Finally, it should be noted that the government of Zimbabwe's drive to indigenization, and the lack of vigor in promoting JVs in the agribusiness sector with foreign firms may have emanated from the dominant position of foreign firms that exists in the economy already. Two characteristics of Zimbabwean agriculture make it distinct from other typical SSACs. Fist, the agricultural sector in Zimbabwe is relatively advanced, and second a major portion of farming is owned and run by white Zimbabweans. Therefore, the need for foreign resources to develop the sector may not be as strong as in other countries. The theoretical proposition posited for this case study need be further examined through its application in other African countries.

Notes

1. The IBDC (Indigenous Business Development Center) is a recently established organization with the objective of promoting small/medium enterprises of black Zimbabweans. Though the membership is estimated to be between 1,500 and 2,000, only about 500 had completed the required formalities and registered by September, 1991.

2. Exchange rate in 1986 was US$1 = Z$1.65. The Z$ has been constantly devalued and current rate (September 1991) is roughly US$1 = Z$3.50.

3. The study defined company ownership as follows:

   -Foreign ownership: 51%-100% of the shares held by foreigners
   -Local ownership: 51%-100% of the shares held by Zimbabwe nationals.
   -Percentage does not add up to 100. No explanation is given in the study.

4. Zimbabwe: A Framework for Economic Reform, 1991-1995, January 1991. Government Printer, Harare.

5. OGIL: 'Open General Import License' is an arrangement which provides a list of products for which no import license is required.

6. Budget Statement 1991, Presented to the Parliament of Zimbabwe. 25 July 1991. pp.4-5.

7. Some companies go around to recruit JV partners. An example is the Industrial Consultancy Services, India. This company represents different Indian companies that produce various machineries and equipment, and that desire a foothold in markets of DCs. According to the Director of the company, while the Indian companies would like to put their machineries and equipment as a contribution in a JV (mainly partial equity/partial payment), with generous credit arrangements, the problem has been the inability of the host partners to raise foreign currency even to meet the minimum down payment required.

8. 'Land Use at Mkwasine', presented on the "Outreach" TV Program of the Zimbabwe Television.

References

ADA (1991). *ADA: Annual Report and Accounts, 1989/90.* Harare.

Batezat, E. et al.(1986). 'The Working Conditions of Female Workers in the Food Processing Industry in Zimbabwe (with special reference to canneries)', *Working Papers No.10.* Harare: Zimbabwe Institute of Development Studies.

Cairns Holdings Ltd. *Annual Report 1990.*

CCFT (1991). Cold Comfort Farm Trust: Development Programme, 1990 Annual Report and 1991 Plans. Harare. (unpublished monograph).

CDC (1991). 'Back to Office Report: RVDC, Zimbabwe. Review Mission 10-12 June, 1991'. July 1991. (unpublished report).

Commercial Agriculture in Zimbabwe, 1990/91. Harare: Modern Farming Publications. 1991.

Hunyani Holdings Ltd. *Annual Report 1990.*

IAD (1991). 'Sustainable Agriculture - What It Implies', *International Agricultural Development.* vol.11 no.3. May/June, 1991. Reading, UK. p.8.

Kunjeku, P.F.(1991). *Project Finance and Technical Support Available to Zimbabwe.* Harare: Confederation of Zimbabwe Industries.

Mashakada, T.(1991). 'What Unique Attributes Do We Have to Perform Wonders with ESAP', *The Financial Gazette*, August 22. Harare.

Maya, S. & Tongoona, H.(1989). 'Ownership Structure of the Manufacturing Sector vol.II. *Consultancy Report NO.9.* Harare: Zimbabwe Institute of Development Studies .

Miles, M.B. & Huberman, A.M.(1984). *Qualitative Data Analysis.* Beverly Hills: SAGE Publication Inc.

Moyo, J.(1991). 'Economic Reform Programme is a Foreign Product', *The Financial Gazette*, September 5. Harare.

Olivine Today, (3rd & 1st Quarters, 1991; 4th, 3rd, 2nd, & 1st Quarters, 1990). Harare.

UNIDO (1991). *Zimbabwe: Investment Guide, PTA.* (draft monograph).

Wilde, R.V.(1991). 'Address by the Director of ZIC and Deputy Governor of the Reserve Bank of Zimbabwe to the ZNCC 1991 Congress on 15 May 1991 at the Victoria Falls'. Harare. (monograph).

Yin, R.K.(1989). *Case Study Research: Design and Methods.* Applied social research methods series. vol.5. Newbury Park: SAGE Publications Inc.

7 Attitudes of UK executives towards JV formation in SSACs: A survey

Introduction

This chapter presents the analysis of data gathered through the questionnaire sent out to senior executives of UK based food and agribusiness companies. 70 questionnaires were mailed, and a total of 54 executives responded of which 37 completed usable questionnaires. The reasons why some executives did not complete the questionnaire are discussed in Chapter 4.

In addition to this introduction, the chapter is organized into 7 sections. In the section following introduction characteristics of the sampled companies based on primary data are described. The subsequent sections present the results of tests of hypotheses with regard to the attitudes of executives of UK based food and agribusiness firms on: a) the different business participation forms; b) the different host partners; c) the importance of the various resources and attributes expected of the host partners; and d) the host country specific entry environment for joint venture (JV) formation. In each section, the objectives of the analysis, test results of the null hypotheses, conclusions and implications of findings are discussed. To test the null hypotheses, the Friedman test and the Mann-Whitney test were applied. The reasons for choosing these tests of significance are discussed in Chapter 4.

The Friedman test is applied in those parts of the analysis where the particular observations are more than two and related. In Friedman test, the k variables to be compared are ranked from 1 to k for each case, and the mean ranks for the variables calculated and compared resulting in a test statistic with approximately a chi-square distribution. (Norusis 1988, Holmes 1974, Dillon et al 1990).

According to Siegel (1956) and Meddis (1984), when 3 or more conditions are to be compared, it is necessary to use a statistical test which will indicate whether there is an over-all difference among the conditions before one picks out any pair of conditions in order to test the significance of the difference between them. Therefore, in sections where the Friedman test resulted in rejecting the null hypothesis, the significant differences between the conditions are tested. For the analyses in sections where the purpose is to identify a group of variables that are considered important, conclusions are drawn from the Friedman tests and a comparison of median scores.

There are two tests available for testing the significance of differences between the conditions where the Friedman procedure resulted in significant differences; namely the Sign test and the Wilcoxon signed-ranks test. (Norusis). According to Siegel, the Wilcoxon signed-ranks test is more powerful than the sign test, as the former incorporates information about the magnitude of the differences, while the latter uses only the direction of the differences between the pairs of conditions. Therefore, the Wilcoxon signed-ranks test is employed.

In those parts of analysis where the specific null hypotheses are concerned with the two groups in the sample, i.e., large and medium/small firms, the Mann-Whitney test is applied. According to Siegel, the Mann-Whitney U test is one of the most powerful of the non-parametric tests, and it is a most useful alternative to the parametric t-test when conditions are not sufficient to use the t-test.

The Mann-Whitney test is used to determine whether median rating levels are the same for the two groups. The statistic used in the Mann-Whitney test is U. The U statistic is the number of times that a score in the group with larger cases precedes a score in the group with smaller cases in the ranking (Siegel). Siegel provides the procedure for computing the value of U for different sample and group sizes, and making decisions based on these values. As the SPSS has been used for this study, there was no need to make computations as proposed by Siegel.

The output from the Mann-Whitney procedure includes the mean rank for each group, the number of cases for each group, the U statistic, the Wilcoxon W, the Z statistic, and an observed significant level. For samples with less than 30 cases, the SPSS produces the exact observed significant level and for larger samples, a Z statistic with its approximate observed significant level. As the reported significant level is used to arrive at a decision for each test, the subsequent tables for the Mann-Whitney tests show the relevant variables, the mean ranks for the groups, and the observed significant levels.

Company characteristics of the sample firms

Length of business experience

The length of business experience is measured in terms of the number of years since the firm had the first business involvement in an African country. Table 7.1 presents the distribution of the two groups of the sample firms and the number of years of experience in English speaking African countries (ESACs): a) 'less than 5 years' or with a relatively little experience, b) 'between 5 to 10 years', or with moderate experience, and c) over 10 years experience, with relatively long experience.

Table 7.1
Length of business experiences of the sample firms in ESACs

Length of experience	Large firms	Medium/ small firms	Total
Less than 5 years	-- --	3 (8%)	14 (8%)
5-10 years	3 (8%)	3 (8%)	6 (16%)
More than 10 years	16 (43%)	12 (33%)	28 (76%)
Total	19 (51%)	18 (49%)	37 (100%)

Of the 37 firms sampled, those with less than 5 years business experience in ESACs were all medium/small firms. In the between 5 and 10 years category the two groups of firms are equally distributed representing 16% of the sample. Two thirds of all the firms have relatively long experience of business in ESACs. Though large firms appear to be longer established in ESACs, the data indicate that the number of medium/small firms is increasing.

Table 7.2 presents the distribution of firms in the sample by type of their current business participation in ESACs.

Table 7.2
Distribution of the sample firms by the type of business involvement in ESACs

Business type	Large firms	Medium/ small firms	Total
Wholly owned manufacturing	11 (30%)	3 (8%)	14 (38%)
Joint manufacturing	8 (22%)	5 (13%)	13 (35%)
Contract farming	3 (8%)	3 (8%)	6 (16%)
Licensing agreements	6 (16%)	1 (3%)	7 (19%)
Management/technical services	9 (24%)	8 (22%)	17 (46%)
Exporting to African countries	12 (32%)	9 (24%)	21 (56%)
Importing from African countries	9 (24%)	6 (16%)	15 (40%)

For the whole sample, operations of firms are highly concentrated in exporting, management/technical services, and importing. However, it can be seen from Table 7.2 that wholly owned subsidiaries (wos) and JVs are not far behind; where respectively 38% and 35% of the firms are involved. The forms of business involvement least utilized by firms are contract farming and licensing. Large firms are highly involved not only in trading activities but also in direct investment types, represented by wos and JVs. On the other hand medium/small firms are less represented in the direct investment types.

Table 7.3 shows the diversity of the forms of business adopted by the sample firms. Involvements in the various business forms ranged between a maximum of 6 and a minimum of 1. 35% of the firms operate in only one business type, and 27% in 2 types. Another 27% have highly diversified involvement, participating in 4 or more of the business types indicated.

Table 7.3
Diversity of business involvement of the sample firms in ESACs

Category	Large firms	Medium/ small firms	Total
In 1 business form	5 (14%)	3 (8%)	13 (35%)
In 2 business forms	5 (14%)	5 (14%)	10 (27%)
In 3 business forms	1 (3%)	3 (8%)	4 (11%)
In 4 business forms	1 (3%)	2 (5%)	3 (8%)
In 5 business forms	6 (16%)	-- --	6 (16%)
In 6 business forms	1 (3%)	-- --	1 (3%)
Total	19 (51%)	18 (49%)	37 (100%)

Extent of JV experience

Here, the extent of JV experience is measured in terms of the number of food and agribusiness JVs that a firm currently has in ESACs. Table 7.4 presents the distribution of firms in the sample in terms of this variable.

Table 7.4
Experience in and intention of joint venturing by the sample firms

Experience/intention	Large firms	Medium/ small firms	Total
1 JV currently	2 (6%)	2 (6%)	4 (11%)
2-3 JVs currently	4 (11%)	2 (6%)	6 (17%)
More than 4 JVs currently	3 (8%)	3 (8%)	6 (17%)
None currently, will consider in the future	4 (11%)	4 (11%)	8 (22%)
None currently, do not find JV appropriate	6 (17%)	6 (17%)	12 (33%)
Total	19 (53%)	17 (47%)	36 (100%)

Of all the sample firms, 45% had some JV experience in ESACs. 33% do not consider JV as a good strategy for doing business in ESACs. A considerable number of firms (22%) do not have any JV at present, but intend to consider them when possibilities arise. By aggregating those that have JVs at present and those that intend to form them in the future, which form 67%, it can be noticed that a considerable portion of the firms have positive attitudes towards joint venturing. This can be further assessed by looking into the level of satisfaction experienced by those firms with current JVs, which is discussed in the following paragraphs.

Level of satisfaction with the JV form

Firms reported the level of their satisfaction in terms of generally satisfied, mixed (satisfaction with some and dissatisfaction with some others), and not at all satisfied. As noted above, 16 firms or about 45% of the sample have some experience of JVs in ESACs. Table 7.5 presents the distribution of the sample firms with JV experience by the level of satisfaction with the JV mode.

Table 7.5
Satisfaction with JVs

Level of satisfaction	Large firms	Medium/ small firms	Total
Generally satisfied	6 (36%)	3 (19%)	9 (56%)
Mixed	3 (19%)	2 (13%)	5 (31%)
Not satisfied	-- (13%)	2 (13%)	2 (13%)
Total	9 (56%)	7 (44%)	16 (100%)

It is interesting to note that the majority of the firms (60%), expressed their general satisfaction with their JVs. Only 12.5% indicated that they are dissatisfied with their JVs, and these two firms are in the medium/small firms category. The evidence indicates that more large firms are satisfied with their JVs than the medium/small firms. Though the above table shows that not all firms with the JV experience are satisfied, the over all indication is still that JVs are popular among the majority of the firms.

Preferred strategy for business participation

Objectives and hypotheses

In this section the perceived appropriateness of the seven different forms of business participation in meeting company objectives are discussed. The specific objectives and the null hypotheses are stated as follows.

There are two objectives: a) to determine which are the most preferred forms of business participation by foreign firms in ESACs; and b) to determine if there is any significant difference in the preferences of large firms and medium/small firms. Corresponding to these objectives the respective null hypotheses are:

> Ho1: There is no difference in the preference of foreign firms between the different forms of business participation.

> Ho2: There is no difference between large firms and medium/small firms in their preferences to the different forms of business participation.

Test results of Ho1: Applying the Friedman test, the seven related variables are ranked and compared. The results of the test are presented in Table 7.6.

Table 7.6
Results of Friedman's test for UK firms' preferences of business participation forms

Business participation form	Mean rank
Wos	4.45
(Foreign) majority JVs	4.30
Co-owned JVs (50-50)	3.58
(Foreign) minority JVs	3.06
Management/technical agreements	4.53
Licensing	3.53
Import/export	4.55

cases	D.F.	significance
33	6	0.0182

The results show that the seven modes of business participation differ in their perceived appropriateness to fulfil company objectives. The observed significance is 1.8%. That is, we can reject the null hypothesis with less that 2% of being wrong in doing so. From this data, we can conclude that executives have different preferences among the alternative business participation forms in ESACs. However, from the above result, we do not know whether there exists significant differences in the ranks between any of the two variables. To determine which differences are responsible for the overall significant result, a multiple comparison using the Wilcoxon signed-ranks test was carried out. (Table 7.7).

Each business participation form (identified as I) is paired and compared with each of the others (identified as II), and the null hypothesis of no difference between their ranks is tested. Decisions arrived at at 5% significance level are also shown on the table. The following major conclusions are drawn from the results shown on the table:

i)   Wos are more preferred than 50/50 JVs and minority JVs.

ii)   Majority JVs are more preferred than 50/50 JVs and minority JVs.

iii)   Coownerhsip (50/50 JVs) are not preferred by executives compared to any of the alternatives.

iv)   Minority JVs are not preferred by executives compared to any of the alternatives.

v)   Management/technical agreements are more preferred compared to minority JVs and licensing.

vi)   Licensing is not preferred by executives in comparison with any of the alternatives.

vii)   Import/export are more preferred than 50/50 JVs, minority JVs, management/technical agreements, and licensing.

Table 7.7
Summary of the Wilcoxon Matched-pairs Signed-Ranks test for business participation strategies

Paired business participation forms			No. of cases where			2-tailed
I	vs	II	II<I	II>I	ties	P
Wos	vs	majority JV	10	9	14	0.9839
Wos	vs	50/50 JV	16	7	10	0.0914
Wos	vs	minority JV	18	8	7	0.0201*
Wos	vs	man./tech. agreements	12	13	8	0.9785
Wos	vs	licensing	19	10	4	0.1415
Wos	vs	import/export	15	13	5	0.4802
Majority JV	vs	50/50 JV	14	3	16	0.0121*
Majority JV	vs	minority JV	19	6	8	0.0027*
Majority JV	vs	man./tech. agreements	9	14	10	0.9152
Majority JV	vs	licensing	17	11	5	0.1035
Majority JV	vs	import/ export	12	16	5	0.4945
50/50 JV	vs	minority JV	12	5	16	0.0929
50/50 JV	vs	man./tech. agreements	7	19	7	0.0552
50/50 JV	vs	licensing	15	11	7	0.9899
50/50 JV	vs	import/export	11	18	4	0.0298*
Minority JV	vs	man./tech. agreements	5	20	8	0.0022*
Minority JV	vs	licensing	8	13	12	0.2736
Minority JV	vs	import/export	8	20	5	0.0051*
Man./tech. agreements vs licensing			13	7	13	0.0290*
Man./tech. agreements vs import/export			10	15	9	0.3395
Licensing	vs	import/export	3	14	16	0.0080*

*Significant at 5%

In summary, the results show that executives tended to have high preferences for wos, majority JVs, and import/export, followed by management/technical agreements, and licensing. The least preferred forms of business participation in ESACs were minority JVs and 50/50 JVs.

Test results of Ho2: The null hypothesis that was tested is that there is no difference in the preferences of large firms and medium/small firms. The results of the Mann-Whitney test, presented on Table 7.8, shows different p values.

Table 7.8
Results of Mann-Whitney test

Business involve mode	Mean ranks Large firms	Medium/ small firms	2-tailed P
Wos	20.39	12.93	0.024*
(Foreign) majority JVs	20.22	13.13	0.029*
Co-owned JVs (50-50)	18.56	15.13	0.291
(Foreign) minority JVs	17.72	16.13	0.618
Management/technical agreements	16.58	18.53	0.558
Licensing agreements	15.61	18.67	0.339
Import/export	17.42	20.67	0.343

* significant at 5%

We observe that in all cases except for wos and (foreign) majority JVs, large P values are indicated. The probability for wos and (foreign) majority JVs, is 2.4% and 2.9% respectively, smaller than the significant level of 5%, and therefore, the null hypothesis of no difference in median can be rejected.

From the above analysis it is concluded that large firms are more inclined to get involved in direct investment, i.e. in the forms of wos and (foreign) majority JVs. However, for co-owned JVs, (foreign) minority JVs, management/technical agreements, licensing agreements, and import/export as the probability indicated is much higher than the significant level, there is no reason to suspect different medians. Therefore, the conclusion arrived at is that the two groups did not have significant differences in the preferability/nonpreferability of the business participation forms mentioned.

Discussion of results

The first analysis resulted in the conclusion that executives tended to have high preferences for wos, majority JVs, and import/export; the least preferred being minority JVs and 50/50 JVs. The reasons for the preference/non-preference for a specific business participation form have been compiled during the follow up interviews. The following paragraphs discuss the explanations for the results of the hypotheses tests.

i) Wos: In comparison with those forms of business participation that require direct investment, namely the three types of JVs, wos faired better in the rankings with the exception of (foreign) majority JVs. During the follow-up interview executives were asked to explain the reasons for their preference or non preference for wos.

The main reasons mentioned by those who prefer wos include:

-The firm has a long standing policy of sole ownership of its subsidiaries. Some firms did not point out any specific reason for this except indicating it has been the tradition;

-Partitioning ownership could bring about conflict with shareholders;

-Corporate objectives are better met through own subsidiaries;

-Bringing in others is troublesome; and

-We only involve others if we cannot do it alone.

Many respondents, however, indicated that the opportunity for establishing wos in many ESACs and other DCs is generally not conducive. Most host governments directly or indirectly pressure for local participation in the venture, which may result in a JV.

ii) JVs: Executives' attitudes towards JVs is found to vary. Some executives show strong preference to JVs in general. The reasons this group of executives gave for preferring JVs include:

-Share in ownership would soften the feeling for nationalism. In many ESACs, foreign firms were generally associated with colonialism, and there still exists the 'them and us' mentality. Local participation would help overcome these and related problems;

-Ventures in sugar plantations and other plantations require long term land commitment, and this is better treated as a contribution by local interests, as the land issue is generally sensitive;

-Local participation generates good will; and

-Using maximum local inputs result in overall lower costs as local manpower and material resources are relatively cheaper.

However, some executives draw a line between majority JVs and 50-50 or minority JVs. Those who prefer majority JVs explained that the main weakness they experienced with 50-50 JVs are: 50-50 JVs result in 'deadlock boards', frequent conflicts, and less commitment by both parties. In some countries, conflicts would call for the interference of the government. For instance, Company A(1) declines any participation in a JV where their share would be on a 50-50 or minority basis. Recently, they had to withdraw from a proposed JV in Nigeria where the local interest wanted the majority control and Company A was offered a 40% share.

Another argument explained by other executives was that besides the loss of management control, minority JVs often do not warrant the effort and the cost. Particularly where the venture is to be located in the far away countries of Africa, the cost could be very high. In comparison, for instance, if the JV were to be located in a neighboring European country a minority JV could be welcomed by these executives.

iii) Management/technical agreements: Those executives who favor the management/technical agreement option had the following main reasons:

-These executives felt that they have specialized services with the required units within their organization to meet the needs of ESACs;

141

-Management/technical services are widely needed in ESACs associated with purchase of machinery, product development, expansion, diversification, etc.;

-Management/technical agreements often follow import/export relations and accompany purchases, licensing and other forms;

-Management/technical services do not require large financial commitments; and

-Management/technical agreement allow flexibility, generally do not involve long term resource commitment, can be provided to small or large projects and often are less affected by political situations in the host country.

iv) Licensing: Among the sampled firms and those interviewed, few firms were involved in licensing agreements. Among those interviewed during the follow-up survey only Company B(2) indicated an experience of licensing in ESACs. Company B has a licensing agreement with an influential, large food firm in Kenya. Though the agreement has run for more than 10 years, the licensor is not satisfied with the arrangement, and considers it a failed relationship. The reasons for the dissatisfaction are:

-The licensee has the exclusive right to sell the products in the whole of Africa. The licensor feels that the firm did not make the right market penetration strategy, and many markets are lost to competitors;

-The firm fails to pay royalties in foreign exchange, as a result of which such funds are kept idle in the bank in local currency;

-The licensee is pressing for permission to export to other non-African markets, mainly to Asian countries, where this is in conflict with the interest of the licensor;

-The licensee has not maintained the high standard of products, and the brand is getting a bad reputation in the market place;

-The licensor have to incur high costs (travel, management time and fees) due to repeated visits to Kenya to sort out problems;

-The licensee is a firm with 'political connections', and has been difficult to deal with.

The licensing experience has made Company B very cautious of arrangements where they do not have majority control. As a general policy they want total ownership of their ventures. JVs are welcome where Company B are assured of management control and where the markets are attractive, such as Eastern European countries and the former USSR. Though foreign exchange shortages, and therefore repatriation of profits are similarly difficult in these countries, they are considered still attractive, as the company has a policy of reinvesting in the host country and count on benefits in the long run due to the large opportunities the markets provide.

v) Import/Export: Many firms in the sample indicated their preference towards import/export participation over the other forms. Even for firms with diversified involvement, import/export is still an important operation. The explanations given by executives during the follow up interview are summarized as: both importation and exportation are easier to start, are testing grounds for the direct investment forms of business, and require less resource commitment, and are relatively less risky than the other alternative business forms. For firms engaged in exporting to ESACs the major attractions to this business forms for them were:

-Risk aversion: payments are immediate while other forms imply future returns which therefore are more uncertain;

-Requires relatively small resource commitment (financial and manpower resources);

-It is ideal to reach small and fragmented markets which characterizes most African markets.

However, the reasons appear to vary between the medium/ small firms and the large firms. Large firms employ importing and exporting in addition to the other business forms. The participation form of some firms, mostly in the medium/small category is limited to import or export. Some of the explanations why they stick to just importing/exporting, and why not they form JVs or wos in ESACs, executives responded as follows:

-They would rather expand in nearby markets (within UK, and Europe);

-Agricultural production and processing, which is the opportunity in ESACs, is not their strength and lack the experience;

-Agricultural production is risky, involving uncertain natural, political, and cultural situations;

-Distance between UK and ESACs would make such an involvement difficult and expensive;

-The UK and European markets are getting more and more competitive, requiring them to update, invest, and further specialize. For example, Company C(3) explained that they had to invest recently £2.5 million to improve their marketing infrastructure, and stay competitive in the UK market.

Though these firms indicated that they are often dissatisfied with their supplies from ESACs, and understand the need for better production processes, machinery, technology, etc., they feel providing these resources is not their priority. Such firms who appear to be content with the purely trading relation have indicated some of the areas of cooperation which they are prepared to consider. These are: advice and consultancy on packaging and handling, market information, technology, standard and quality control, and in some cases transportation. They expect the supplier side to take the initiative, the investment required.

Major implications of these findings

-Avoiding barriers on exercising management control and majority ownership by foreign firms is likely to enhance foreign investment in ESACs;

-Among the three alternatives commonly applied in joint venturing, namely (foreign) majority JVs, coownership, and (foreign) minority JVs, only the foreign majority owned option is strongly preferred; and therefore indicate the need to review policies towards promoting (foreign) majority JVs. This result is consistent with the findings of a previous study undertaken by Hewaidy (1988). Hewaidy, in his study of host government control of foreign manufacturing companies in Egypt, surveyed opinions of foreign company executives and government officials about the preferability of the three forms of investment (foreign wos, foreign majority JVs and foreign minority JVs) for meeting company objectives. His findings with regard the opinion of foreign company executives was that, wos and foreign majority JVs are preferred rather than minority JVs.

-Findings from previous studies (e.g. Beamish 1988) indicate that foreign firms' participation in JVs in DCs has been in most cases on the majority or minority basis rather than on the 50/50 basis. However, among the two the minority JVs appear to predominate. Beamish cites Franko's findings that in 71 DC-based JVs of 8 American firms, in none of the JVs had the firms a majority equity interest. The findings of this study that executives of foreign firms do not favor minority or 50/50 interests in JVs imply that such forms are taken up by foreign firms because of regulations or other pressures by host countries.

-The need of resources in short supply in SSACs such as capital and technology is more likely to come from large firms rather than medium/small firms.

Preferred host partners for JV formation

Objectives and hypotheses

This section discusses the perceived preference among prospective host partners by company executives for forming JVs in ESACs. The objectives set for this section are: a) to determine which is the most preferred type of host firm as partner in a JV; and b) to determine if there is any significant difference in the preferences of large firms and medium/small firms between host partners for JV formation. The null hypotheses are stated as follows:

Ho1: There is no significant difference in the preferences of foreign firms between the different types of host partners.

Ho2: There is no significant difference between large firms and medium/small firms in their preferences to the different types of host partners.

Test results Ho1 : The scores given to each type of host partner on the scale of 5 are the related variables of interest. Accordingly, therefore, the 5 variables are ranked and compared.

Table 7.9
Results of Friedman's test for UK firms' rankings of host partners

Types of host partners	Mean rank
Privately owned firms	4.20
State owned firms	2.41
Co-operatives	1.80
Public companies	3.55
Foreign firms	3.04

Cases	D.F.	significance
28	4	0.0000

The results on Table 7.9 show that the observed significance level is extremely small, and therefore, the null hypothesis can be rejected. Based on this data, it is concluded that the five types of host partners differ in their perceived suitability as capable host partners to form JVs. However, from the above result, we do not know whether there exists significant differences in the ranks between any of the two variables. To determine which differences are responsible for the overall significant result, a multiple comparison using the Wilcoxon signed-ranks test was carried out. (Table 7.10).

146

Table 7.10
Summary of the Wilcoxon Matched-pairs Signed-Ranks test
for host partners

| Paired host partner types | | | No. of cases where | | | 2-tailed |
I vs II			II<I	II>I	Ties	P
Privately owned firms	vs	state owned firms	25	3	2	0.0003*
Privately owned firms	vs	cooperatives	26	1	2	0.0000*
Privately owned firms	vs	public companies	15	4	11	0.0070*
Privately owned firms	vs	foreign firms	18	4	7	0.0016*
State owned firms	vs	cooperatives	14	3	12	0.0217*
State owned firms	vs	public companies	2	20	8	0.0035*
State owned firms	vs	foreign firms	9	16	4	0.1218
Cooperatives	vs	public companies	2	22	5	0.0007*
Cooperatives	vs	foreign firms	5	19	4	0.0119*
Public companies	vs	foreign firms	11	8	10	0.1590

*Significant at 5%.

Each host partner type (identified as I) is paired and compared with each of the others (identified as II), and the null hypothesis of no difference between their ranks is tested. Decisions arrived at at 5% significance level are also shown on the table. The following conclusions are drawn from the results shown on the table:

i)   Privately owned firms are more preferred to any of the other types of host partners.

ii)   State owned firms are more preferred to cooperatives, and less preferred to privately owned firms and public companies.

iii)   Cooperatives are not preferred to any of the other types of host partners.

iv) Public companies are more preferred compared to state owned firms and cooperatives, and less preferred compared to privately owned firms.

v) Foreign firms in the host country are more preferred when compared with cooperatives only.

To summarize, it can be concluded that privately owned firms are the most suitable host partners for foreign firms, followed by public companies. The least preferred host partners are cooperatives. State owned firms and foreign firms are in between.

Test results of Ho2: It is of interest to find out if there are differences in the preferences of the different modes by large and medium/small firms. The null hypothesis that there is no difference in the preferences of large firms and medium/small firms was tested. Results of the Mann-Whitney test presented in Table 7.11 show different p values. We observe that in all cases large P values are indicated, and therefore, there is no reason to suspect different medians; and the null hypothesis is not rejected.

Table 7.11
Results of Mann-Whitney test

| | Mean ranks | | |
	Large firms	Medium/ small firms	2-tailed P
Private sector firms	16.00	16.00	1.000
State-owned firms	16.69	14.41	0.409
Cooperatives	7.60	13.40	0.173
Public (share) companies	16.56	14.29	0.468
Foreign firms	15.47	14.42	0.736

The data support the conclusion that large firms and medium/small firms agree on the suitability/non-suitability of the different types of host partners for joint venturing.

Privately owned firm partners were considered to be the most suitable for JV formation in ESACs. Public companies were the next preferred, while cooperatives were the least. The reasons why some are more preferred than others were compiled during the follow-up interview, and summarized as follows:

i) Private sector firms: The preference for private sector firms is often expressed in comparison with the state sector firms. The reasons for the preference for private sector firms are:

-There is a better congruity of objectives, mainly profit orientation;

-Employees are generally more motivated than those in the state sector; and

-There is less pressure for non-business influences.

Though the preference for private sector firms is strong, it is by no means unanimous. There are some firms which some times prefer other types of firms rather than private sector firms particularly in some DCs. For instance Company A, if they have to go into a JV, they seek for passive partners. Cooperatives and public companies fulfil this condition better than private sector firms which generally tend to seek dominant and active part in the JV. Further, private sector firms in some ESACs are relatively unstable and volatile compared to state sector and public companies. State sector firms, cooperatives and public companies enjoy better 'respectability' in some communities/countries than private sector firms.

ii) State sector firms: Though most executives interviewed would avoid state sector firms as partners, they find themselves to consider them as partners whether they like it or not. Many examples of JVs mentioned by executives were with the state-owned firms. During the follow-up interview executives gave the following reasons why they participated in JVs with the state sector:

-In many ESACs land is controlled by government, and where agri-production is involved it is convenient to have a state owned firm as partner;

-Where investment opportunities are good but the prospective partner is state-owned firm;

-Private sector firms which are capable to contribute towards JVs in ESACs are relatively scarce;

-Since independence, a lot of resources have gone into the state sector mainly by way of nationalization, and therefore state-owned firms are relatively more capable as partners.

Executives gave the main reasons for avoiding partnership with state-owned firms as:

-State owned firms are bureaucratic and decisions are slow;

-They are reluctant to meet commitments, particularly financial. 'They are in the habit of running out of money', is how one interviewee drew from his experience.

-They tend to introduce divergent objectives (social, and political influences), and less committed to profit making.

Relatively large, more experienced and diversified firms appear to be more accommodating towards state-owned firms.

iii)Cooperatives: During the follow-up interviews it was found out that executives that indicated preference to cooperatives are few and exceptions. The main reasons for the non-preference of cooperatives were given by executives as follows:

-Cooperatives lack resources, particularly financial and manpower resources, and managerial and technical skills;

-Cooperatives in ESACs are relatively new and their management inexperienced (relative to the countries of Asia and Latin America). They are poorly and loosely organized, and often call for interference by government, which makes a JV management complicated;

-They emphasis social aspects than profit making;

-Difficult to maintain high quality and standard products due to diversity and scattered nature of production.

In one exceptional case cooperatives are presented as good host partners. Company A values the management and control of the venture as the highest priority. Therefore, in the circumstances where they cannot establish wos but JVs are the only possibility the strategy is to seek for a passive host partner. According to their experiences, cooperatives and public sector firms were more passive than private sector firms.

iv) Public companies: Some of the reasons given for favoring public companies are similar to those of private sector firms. However, some executives consider public companies as more stable and sometimes as more 'respectable' than private sector firms in some ESACs where private sector firms are often inexperienced and small.

v) Foreign firms: Explanations differed in the preference shown to foreign firms in the host country. Those few which are in favor indicated that there will be better understanding of objectives, would be able to contribute substantially towards the JV, their knowledge of the local situation will be advantageous. However, many seem not to go for foreign firms as partners because:

-Foreign firms are often competitors internationally;

-Of the fact that they are also foreign, and therefore, do not meet the 'national' aspect of the JV which could be essential to the formation of the venture;

-They generally have similar resources as the incoming foreign firm.

Major implications of the findings

-The finding that foreign firms strongly favor private sector firms than state-owned firms as partners in a JV supports the conclusions of various studies in the JV literature (e.g. Raveed and Renforth 1983, Beamish 1988).

-The strong preference for private firms followed by public companies on the one hand, and the weak preference for cooperatives and state-owned firms imply that privatization could be a vehicle for attracting foreign firms in to partnership for JV in ESACs.

-The predominance of state-owned firms in particular and state intervention in general could be linked to the low occurrences of JVs in ESACs.

Resources and attributes sought

Objectives and hypotheses

This section presents the analysis of the perceived importance of the 10 different attributes that may be expected from the prospective host partner by the prospective foreign partner in forming a JV. These resources and attributed were identified in the JV literature review (see Chapter 3). They are financial contributions, management/technical skills, marketing channels, local influence/contacts, local technology, machinery & equipment, offices and buildings, cheap labor, supply of raw materials, and access to agricultural land.

The objectives are: a) to determine which of the resource attributes sought by foreign firms from prospective host partners are critical; and b) to determine if there is any significant difference in the evaluation of the resources and attributes by large firms and medium/small firms. The null hypotheses are stated as follows:

Ho1: There is no significant difference in the evaluation of foreign firms between the ten resources and attributes expected from the prospective host partners.

Ho2: There is no significant difference between the evaluations of the ten resources and attributes expected of host partners by large firms and medium/small firms.

Test Results of Ho1: The null hypothesis tested was that there is no difference in the importance of the different attributes. The results of the Friedman test are given in Table 7.12.

Table 7.12
Results of Friedman's test

Resources and attributes	Mean rank
Financial contributions	6.92
Management/technical skills	6.92
Marketing channels	6.54
Local influence/contacts	8.13
Local technology	4.50
Machinery & equipment	3.77
Offices and buildings	4.83
Cheap labor	3.58
Supply of raw materials	6.06
Access to agricultural land	3.75

Cases	D.F.	significance
24	9	0.0000

From Table 7.12, it can be observed that the 10 attributes differ in their perceived importance. The observed significance level is extremely small, and therefore, the null hypothesis of no difference can be rejected.

Test Results of Ho2: The null hypothesis that there is no difference in the preferences of large firms and medium/small firms was tested. The Mann-Whitney test results showed that in all cases large P values are indicated. Therefore, there is no reason to suspect different medians and the null hypothesis is not rejected. The data supports the conclusion that there is no difference between the opinions of executives of large firms and medium/small firms with regard the importance or resources and attributes expected of the prospective host partners.

153

Since the need for resources and attributes by foreign firms differs, it is necessary to identify those which are more important or critical to the decision to form a JV. By critical is meant that the host partner should be particularly strong in these resources, the lack of which would result in the disinterest of the foreign partner. The scale was constructed with five points, 4 meaning 'very important', and 5 'most important'. The resources with a median score of 4 and above, which imply relatively high importance to the particular resource, are to be considered critical. On this basis, five resources and attributes were considered critical; namely, local influences/contacts, management/technical skills, marketing channels, financial contributions and access to agricultural land. (Table 13).

Table 7.13
Executives' opinions regarding the importance of various resources

Resources and attributes	Most important					Not important at all	M
	5	4	3	2	1	0*	
Financial contributions	9	4	9	3	1	--	4
Management/technical skills	10	11	8	--	2	1	4
Marketing channels	8	11	5	5	1	--	4
Local influence/contacts	17	9	3	1	--	--	5
Local technology	2	4	9	10	3	1	3
Machinery & equipment	4	1	8	6	8	3	2
Offices and buildings	3	5	9	9	2	2	3
Cheap labor	--	2	10	7	7	3	2
Supply of raw materials	11	1	7	6	2	3	3
Access to agricultural land	6	3	3	3	2	13	4

0* not applicable, M = median

A Median score of 5 for local influence/contacts is particularly high, while the other 4 critical resources have the same median score of 4. On the other hand, the other 5 attributes scored less than the critical mark though there are some variations between them.

The reasons why some of these resources and attributes are considered more important than others was compiled through follow-up interviews and summarized as follows.

i) Local influence/contacts: The attribute regarded to be the most important is local influence/contacts of the host partner. Though this attribute of the host partner may not be sufficient in itself as a contribution to form a JV, it is however, an essential one. According to the executives interviewed the host partner should:

-Have been operating for a reasonably long time to have developed widespread contacts, particularly in government circles, banks, etc.;

-Be able to handle red tape and the various procedures of setting up a business;

-Be knowledgeable of the regulations, laws, and customs of the community/country. For instance, in operations where agri-production is involved, the local partner should be able to influence, among others, the 'chiefs' who have a strong influence in the community; and

-Be a firm with a good reputation in the community/country.

ii) Financial contributions: Financial capability of the host partner is considered critical by executives. The explanation given by some executives interviewed include:

-Major disputes in JV formation is related to the extent of commitments of the partners. Considerable financial outlay increases the commitment of the partner to the JV;

-Host partners have better access to raise local currency from national banks;

-Local currency is important to meet particularly working capital requirements (to procure inputs and meet salaries and other recurrent costs).

Some executives indicated their desire of the host partner to commit not only substantial amount of local currency, but also foreign currency. Generally the foreign partner is required to provide the machinery & equipment, technology and technical skills. According to the executives, the foreign partner is often expected to contribute a disproportionately higher share of the total investment.

iii) Management/technical skills: Management/ technical skills as a contribution of the host partner are regarded as important for the following reasons:

- These skills are crucial to the success of the JV. Their local origin and knowledge would help in quick adoption of technology within the venture;

- The alternative, which is recruiting from the home country of the foreign partner or from a third country is expensive;

- Lack of such skill may imply the need for an extensive training program, which is expensive and time consuming.

iv) Marketing channels: The importance of marketing channels was recognized in three different aspects by respondents interviewed:

- Generally, the host partner is expected to have set up the input and supplies channels;

- If production is for the domestic market, the host partners' market infrastructure - stores, outlets, distributors, transportation facilities, sales force are regarded important, and

- Alternatively, if the production is for export, foreign partner executives feel that their firms are better placed to handle the export infrastructure.

v) Supply of raw materials and access to land: Supply of raw materials is an area where the host partner is expected to be strong. For many foreign firms, the strength of the host partner in production/supply of agri-products is the core of the business partnership. The importance of this attribute is further strengthened by the general reluctance of foreign firms to engage in direct primary agri-production. For instance, with regard to access to land, many executives feel that it is a very sensitive issue, and they generally avoid any direct involvement. Only a few firms with long established business interests, such as sugar plantations, regard access to land as an important attribute of the host partner.

vi) Resources and attributes of low importance: The attachment of low importance to local technology, machinery and equipment is not surprising, as the foreign firm is generally better placed to contribute these resources. Some executives indicated that they are aware of some efforts in ESACs for adopting appropriate technology. If such opportunities exist, they are ready to consider them as a contribution of the host partner, as this may generally mean low costs of production. With regard to machinery and equipment, the foreign firm might be in a possession of these resources in whole or in part. Where machinery and equipment are to be procured from third parties, the host partner should be ready to contribute to the cost of the acquisition. Office and buildings fail to be a major concern for foreign firms.

Cheap labor is among the least important contributions expected of the host partner. Reasons mentioned include:

-Labor is readily available, and as such cannot be considered a contribution of a particular host partner;

-Labor costs are more or less levelling off between countries, and between regions within a particular country. Therefore, labor conditions are not among the major factors that influence investment decisions.

Implications of findings

-The importance of local influence/contacts may emanate from the general cultural differences and the often close relation between political positions and business interests in ESACs. The political changes that are taking place in many ESACs might decrease the importance of this factor.

-The low importance of unskilled labor (cheap labor) indicate that labor cost as a factor to attract foreign investment in ESACs may be questionable.

-The high importance for management/technical skills indicate that foreign firms are interested in the quality of the manpower available (trained and skilled), rather than unskilled labor. This has implications for manpower training for ESACs.

-Foreign firms attach importance to the host partners financial contributions mainly to meet local cost (working capital), as this may account a substantial portion of the whole capital outlay in the agri-production, processing and marketing process. Access to favorable credit facilities for prospective host firms is likely to be an important factor for attracting foreign firm partners.

-The situation with access to agri-land resulted in two distinct attitudes: from firms which are interested in agricultural production it is of utmost importance. However, many firms were very reluctant to participate in direct agri-production, and emphasis on secondary and tertiary operations. Access to land, for example in the form of concessions to foreign interest is likely to draw more foreign investment to ESACs.

Though these resources and attributes have been studied previously as cited in the literature review (e.g. Stopford and Wells 1972, Raveed and Renforth, Beamish 1987, Davidson 1982), there has been no attempt to identify the critical ones. These findings show the direction of policy action required so that host partners are better prepared in order to attract foreign JV partners.

Host country specific factors in JV formation

Objectives

In this section we discuss the perceived level of satisfaction/ dissatisfaction of executives with the different host country specific entry factors in the JV formation process. Factors have been identified from previous literature (see Chapter 3) to be important determinants of a foreign company executives' decision to form JVs in DCs. Further, these factors were verified through a pilot study involving in-depth personal interviews conducted during the early stage of this research (see Chapter 5), and finally 23 important factors were identified. Thus, executives were asked to indicate the level of satisfaction/dissatisfaction with each variable in their decision to form or not to form a JV in ESACs on a scale of 1 to 4; 4 representing 'very satisfied', 1 very dissatisfied', and 0 for 'not applicable'.

The two objectives for the analysis in this section are a) to identify the particular host country specific factors that are regarded generally satisfactory, and those that are regarded generally not satisfactory for JV formation in ESACs; and b) to determine if there is any significant difference in the evaluation of entry factors by large and medium/small firm executives.

Distinguishing between those factors which are generally perceived as satisfactory and may not cause a hindrance to foreign firms to form JVs and those factors which are perceived as generally unsatisfactory is thought to be important to develop appropriate JV promotion policies. Due to the large number of variables considered and the relatively small size of the sample, the use of the Friedman test in this case will not be appropriate. Instead, the mean rank of the variables is used to generate categories. (Table 7.14).

The variables are further examined in two ways: first, they are arranged according to their ranks and the top 8 (generally satisfactory), the middle 7 (probably tolerable), and the bottom 8 (generally unsatisfactory) are identified. Secondly, they are grouped into 5 generic factors by putting together those with common characteristics. Thus, the entry factors regrouped into generic factors, and evaluated as 'generally satisfactory', 'generally unsatisfactory', and 'probably tolerable', are presented in Table 7.15.

Discussion of results

i) Political and policy oriented factors: As can be seen from Table 7.15 among the political and policy oriented factors, only political situation is considered generally satisfactory. This is a surprising result as 'political instability' has been identified among the major barriers of foreign investment in DCs. (Poynter 1982, Knowles and Mathur 1989, Greene and Villanueva 1990, Bennell 1990). As the executives were asked to respond to the question in relation to their 'most recent experience with JV formation in ESACs' it can be understood that the countries they considered for JVs are those that enjoy some political and economic stability. During the follow-up interviews, executives who indicated a degree of satisfaction with political situation were asked to explain their response and their explanations fall into three categories:

159

Table 7.14
Ranks for JV entry factors

Entry factors	Mean rank	(rank)
The application & approval process of establishing a JV	12.11	(10)
Ease of importations of raw materials, machinery & parts	11.66	(15)
Domestic raw materials supplies	14.43	(2)
Price regulations on inputs	9.84	(22)
Price regulations on final products	11.80	(13)
Ease of employing foreign staff	10.95	(17)
Availability of host capable partners capable	11.73	(14)
Availability of management skills	12.23	(9)
Protection from nationalization	12.07	(11)
Profit and capital repatriation	10.64	(19)
Banking & financial facilities	13.20	(5)
Efficiencies in executing business operations	13.14	(7)
Host country market size and prospect of expansion	13.91	(3)
Availability of skilled manpower	10.61	(20)
Availability of cheap labor	12.86	(8)
Availability of information on potential investment projects	8.52	(23)
Business ethics practiced (absence of bribes, nepotism, etc.)	10.86	(18)
Government incentives provided	11.39	(16)
Company tax rates	10.20	(21)
Political situation (peaceful & stable environment)	13.80	(4)
Work ethics (workers discipline, productivity, etc.)	14.84	(1)
Infrastructure (ports, transport, telephone, telex, etc.)	13.16	(6)
Regulations on management-employee relations	12.05	(12)

Table 7.15
Evaluation entry determinants arranged in categories

Entry factors	GS*	PT*	GU*
Political & policy oriented factors			
Political situation	X		
Price regulations on inputs		X	
Company tax rates			X
Profit and capital repatriation			X
Ease of employing foreign staff			X
Government incentives provided			X
The application & approval process		X	
Protection from nationalization		X	
Price regulations on final products		X	
Ease of importations of raw materials, etc.		X	
Economic and market oriented factors			
Domestic raw materials supplies	X		
Host country market size & prospect of expansion	X		
Banking & financial facilities	X		
Infrastructure	X		
Availability of information on potential projects			X
Availability of capable host partners		X	
Manpower oriented factors			
Availability of cheap labor	X		
Availability of management skills		X	
Availability of skilled manpower			X
Regulations on management/employee relations		X	
Cultural oriented factors			
Work ethics	X		
Efficiencies in executing business operations	X		
Business ethics practiced			X

---

*GS = generally satisfactory, PT = probably tolerable, and GU = generally unsatisfactory.

-They have been in business in ESACs for a long time, and generally have learned how to cope up with political problems;

-Political problems in most countries they intend JVs have not been serious to affect their business plans;

-As most political instabilities are a result of poverty, unemployment, and lack of economic development they felt that they can contribute to stability by their business involvement in such countries.

On the other hand, 5 factors in the political and policy oriented category, i.e., price regulations on inputs, company tax rates, profit and capital repatriation, ease of employing foreign staff, and government incentives provided are considered as generally unsatisfactory. These are consistent with the previous literature except for government incentive. The effectiveness of incentives to attract foreign firms were considered doubtful. (Barry 1991, Bennell). The data leads to the conclusion that changes in these group of factors are relatively important to attract foreign partners for JVs. The other 4 factors, i.e., the application and approval process, protection from nationalization, price regulation in final products, and ease of importation of raw materials did not fall on either of the two extremes, and may not be barriers to JV formation.

ii) Economic and market oriented factors: Four of the 6 factors grouped under economic and market oriented factors are found to be generally satisfactory by executives. The opinion with regard host country market size and prospect of expansion seem to defy the fact that markets in most ESACs are small, and therefore unattractive. This result is also inconsistent with the literature, the findings of the pilot study and results of the analysis reported earlier in this chapter, which stress the importance of the host country market. From the discussions with executives, the possible explanations for this result include:

-Most of the firms have based their business operations in ESACs on external markets (export), and host markets have been of secondary importance; and therefore their reply has been 'not applicable'; and

-Though individual host markets may be small, executives tend to view markets regionally, and they has seen these markets developing albeit slowly.

Many executives are of the opinion that there is a lack of information on potential investment project in ESACs. This implies that preparing and marketing investible projects would be an important strategy to attract foreign partners.

iii)Other factors: Among those grouped under manpower oriented factors only availability of cheap labor is considered satisfactory. This factor however, is found to be not critically important in earlier analysis in this chapter in attracting foreign partners for JVs. Lack of skilled manpower is considered more acute than lack of management skills. In the cultural oriented factors executives indicated their dissatisfaction with regard to 'business ethics practiced', the major components of which are bribery and nepotism. The other two in this category namely 'work ethics' and 'efficiencies in executing business operations' are found to be generally satisfactory.

With regard to finding out if there are differences in the opinion expressed by executives of the two groups of firms, i.e. large and medium/small firms, the null hypothesis tested. The results of the Mann-Whitney test shows that in all cases except for 'business ethics', large P values are indicated. Therefore, for all the other factors, there is no reason to suspect different medians, and the null hypothesis is not rejected. With regard to business ethics, it can be concluded that large firms consider such practices as bribery and nepotism less of a problem than medium/small firms.

Summary and some implications of findings

In this chapter, the data collected through the questionnaire with regard to the opinions and attitudes of Executives of UK based agribusiness firms were analyzed. The results were presented in four sections which are summarized in the following paragraphs.

Preferred strategy for business participation

The findings showed that executives have different preferences among the alternative business participation forms in ESACs. Executives of foreign firms preferred wos, majority JVs and import/export compared to the other business participation forms. The least preferred forms were minority JVs and 50/50 JVs. Both groups, executives of large firms and medium/small firms, were in agreement about the preferability/non-preferability of all forms except with regard wos and (foreign) majority JVs. Large firms are more inclined to involve in direct investment, i.e. in the modes of (foreign) majority JVs and wos than medium/small firms.

From these findings, the following implications for policy were noted:

-Avoiding barriers on exercising management control and majority ownership by foreign firms is likely to enhance foreign investment in ESACs;

-The need of resources in short supply in ESACs such as capital and technology is more likely to come from large firms rather than medium/small firms.

Preferred host partners for JV formation

The analysis showed that the five types of host partners, private sector firms, state-owned firms, cooperatives, public companies, and foreign firms differ in their perceived suitability as capable host partners to form JVs. The order of suitability was: private firms, public companies, foreign firms, and state-owned firms; and the least being cooperatives. It was also found out that large firms and medium/small firms agree on the suitability/non-suitability of the different types of host partners for joint venturing.

These findings have two major implications:

-The high preferences for private firms and public companies and the relatively low preferences for state-owned firms and cooperatives imply that privatization could be a vehicle for attracting foreign firms in to partnership for JV in ESACs.

-The predominance of state-owned firms in particular and state intervention in general could be linked to the low occurrences of JVs in ESACs.

Resources and attributes sought by foreign firms

The resources and attributes that were found to be critical, i.e., those with a median value of 4 and above were: local influences/contacts, management/technical skills, marketing channels, financial contributions and access to agricultural land. Further, it was also found to exist no significant difference between the opinions of executives of large firms and medium/small firms with regard the importance of resources and attributes expected of the prospective host partners.

Major implications of these findings were:

-The importance shown for local influence/contacts may emanate from the general cultural differences and the often close relation between political positions and business interests in ESACs. As the political changes and privatization policies take root in ESACs, the importance of these attributes is likely to decrease.

-The low scores for cheap labor indicate that cheap labor as a factor to attract foreign investment in ESACs is questionable.

-The relatively high score for management/technical skills indicate that foreign firms are interested in the quality of the manpower (trained and skilled) available, rather than unskilled labor.

-Foreign firms attach importance to the host partners financial contributions mainly to meet local cost (working capital), as this may account a substantial portion of the whole capital outlay in the agri-production, processing and marketing process. Therefore, provision of generous credit facilities to prospective host partners is likely to enhance their capability to attract foreign partners.

-Some firms were reluctant to engage in direct agri-production, the main reason being the sensitive nature of the land question in ESACs. Land concessions, where this does not displace settled local communities, could encourage foreign firms to enter JVs in direct agricultural production activities.

The major objectives of this section was to identify the factors that could be barriers for JV entry by foreign firms. Accordingly, the factors that fall under the bottom 1/3 rankings were identified. These were: price regulations on inputs, company tax rates, profit and capital repatriation, ease of employing foreign staff, and government incentives provided, lack of information on potential investment projects, lack of skilled manpower, business ethics practiced.

The evaluations by the two groups of executives did not differ significantly except in the case of 'business ethics'. A further examination of the data by comparing the median values for the two group lead to the conclusion that medium/small firms find business ethical practices more problematic than their larger counterparts.

The major implications of the findings are summarized as follows:

-Most of the factors with dissatisfaction are under political and government oriented category which implies that they can be corrected with government action.

-Lack of information on potential investment project in ESACs implies that preparing and marketing investible projects would be an important strategy to attract foreign partners.

-The situation with response to business ethics supports our previous finding that large firms are more likely to go for JVs in SSACs than medium/small firms.

Notes

1. Company A: is a code given to one of the companies surveyed. The company is among the largest privately owned corporations in the world.

2. Company B: is a large company specializing in the manufacture of cereal breakfast foods. The company has several subsidiaries in different parts of the world, exports to 74 countries and employs about 2,400 people.

3. Company C: is a small firm that is engaged in importing and distributing fruits and vegetables in the UK market. Besides direct importing, the company also provides consultancy and advice in transportation, marketing, packaging, production and quality control.

References

Barry, F.(1991). 'Industrialisation Strategies for Developing Countries: Lessons from the Irish Experience', *Development Policy Review.* vol.9 no.1 pp.85-98.

Beamish, P.W.(1988). *Multinational Joint Ventures in Developing Countries.* Dorset: Routledge.

_____, (1987). 'Joint Ventures in Less Developed Countries: Partner Selection & Performance', *Management International Review.* vol.27 no.1. pp.23-37.

Bennel, P.(1990). 'British Industrial Investment in sub-Saharan Africa: Corporate Responses to Economic Crisis in 1980s', *Development Policy Review.* vol.8 no.2. pp.155-77.

Davidson, W.H.(1982). *Global Strategic Management.* New York: John Wiley and Sons.

Dillon, W.R. et al.(1990). *Marketing Research in a Marketing Environment.* 2nd edition. Boston: Richard D Irwin, Inc.

Greene, J. and Villaneuva, D.(1990). 'Determinants of Private Investment in Less Developed Countries', *Finance & Development.* December. pp.40-42.

Hewaidy, A.M.(1988). Host Government Control of Foreign Manufacturing Companies: The Egyptian Experience. Unpublished PhD Thesis. University of East Anglia.

Holmes, C.(1974). 'A Statistical Evaluation of Rating Scales', *Journal of the Market Research Society.* Vol.16 no.2. pp.87-108.

Knowles, L.L. and Mathur, I.(1989). 'Joint Venture Strategies for Marketing in China', *Journal of International Consumer Marketing.* vol.2 no.1. pp.37-54.

Meddis, R.(1984). *Statistics Using Ranks: a Unified Approach.* Oxford: Basil Blackwell Publisher Ltd.

Norusis, M.J.(1988). *SPSS/PC+ V2.0 Base Manual.* Chicago: SPSS, Inc.

Poynter, T.A.(1982). 'Government Intervention in Less Developed Countries: the Experience of Multinational Companies', *Journal of International Business Studies.* Spring-Summer. pp.9-25.

Raveed, S.R. & Renforth, W.(1983). 'Sate Enterprise-Multinational Corporation Joint Ventures: How Well Do They Meet Both Partners' Needs?', *Management International Review.* vol. 1 Part 1. pp.47-57.

Siegel, A.(1956). *Non-parametric Tests for the Behavioural Sciences.* New York: McGraw-Hill Book Company, Inc.

Stopford, J.M. & Wells, L.T.(Jr.) (1972). *Managing the Multinational Enterprise.* New York: Basic Books.

8 Summary of findings, conclusions and recommendations

Introduction

This chapter presents a summary of the research findings and a discussion of their implications for policy regarding joint venturing in the agribusiness sector in sub-Saharan African countries (SSACs). The chapter is organized in to seven sections. Section 1 outlines the research problem and its significance. Section 2 is an overview of the research design and methodology. Section 3 summarizes the major findings and their implications for policy for the promotion of joint ventures (JVs) in the agribusiness sector in SSACs. Sections 4 and 5 respectively present the conclusion and recommendations, and the contributions of the study. In section 6, some limitations of the study are summarized; and finally, areas for further research are outlined in section 7.

The research problem and its significance

Among the major problems of agribusiness development in SSACs is the lack of capital, technology and skills to improve production, manufacture, diversify and market agro-based products. During the last decade, SSACs have experienced declining foreign investment, and declining foreign currency earnings for their exports, consisting mainly of primary or semi-processed products.

In most SSACs JVs have been adopted as a major strategy as a means of acquiring scarce resources such as capital, technology, skills and market access. The JV literature, however, has given little space to the strategy of

169

joint venturing in the region of sub-Saharan Africa, even less so to the agribusiness sector of the region. The research question was, therefore, what factors determine the formation of JVs in the food and agribusiness sector in SSACs between foreign firms and local host firms, and what can be done to promote such JVs.

The major objectives of the study were a) to examine the JV entry environment in a selected African country; b) to determine which forms of market entry were preferred by foreign firms with regard to SSACs; c) to determine the preferences of foreign firms as regards to the types of host partners (state, private, public, and others); d) to determine the most important (critical) resources sought by foreign firms from host partners; e) to identify host country specific factors that were perceived as barriers to enter SSACs for JV formation; f) to find out if large firms and medium/small firms differed in their attitudes towards JV formation in SSACs.

This study dealt with the food and agribusiness sector with regards to SSACs, and this has significance both empirically and theoretically. Empirically, given the fact of declining food output in most countries of sub-Saharan Africa, high population growth and urbanization, declining foreign investment, the increasingly competitive environment in the international market place, and the general preference shown for the JV mode by governments in SSACs, tackling issues that inhibit this development are timely and very important. Theoretically, research on JVs in the generic form has focused on the manufacturing sector, and it has been doubtful whether prior studies have properly addressed the particular characteristics of agribusiness. Further, many previous studies of JVs characterized a foreign firm partner as an MNC (or a TNC). This study attempted to identify the possible differences in attitudes and propensities to enter into JVs in the agribusiness sector in SSACs by distinguishing between two sets of foreign firms: large firms and medium/small firms.

Summary of research design and methodology

A mixed research design comprising a case study and a survey study was adopted for the study. Preceding the case and survey studies, a pilot survey was conducted with the main objectives of better understanding of the particular characteristics of the agribusiness sector, and identifying the relevant variables for the data collection instruments. Four instruments were used to collect data: an interview guide for the pilot study, a case study protocol for the case study, a questionnaire for the mail survey, and an interview schedule for the follow-up interview.

Explaining the JV formation environment in an African country setting was basically exploratory and required collection and examination of a lot of data, and from various sources. In such situation where as many data as possible need be collected and examined the more appropriate strategy is the case study strategy. Therefore, the case study method was used for the study of an African country, Zimbabwe. The design adopted was the single-case (embedded) design. By applying a well designed case study this study has broken new ground towards reliability and validity of the case study technique.

After evaluating the pros and cons of conducting only mail interviews or personal interviews, a combination of mail questionnaire and personal interview methods were considered more appropriate to get the optimum result from the survey of UK executives. In designing the questionnaire, a 5-point semantic differential scale has been used. The questionnaire was pretested with five senior executives from five UK based agribusiness firms.

A list containing the research population of interest, i.e., 'executives of UK based food and agribusiness firms with business interests in English-speaking African countries (ESACs)' was not readily available. Therefore, a list of such firms had to be compiled from various sources over the duration of the research period up to the survey. Following the practice from similar studies, employee number was used as the criterion to classify the sample firms by size. Firms with employee numbers of 500 and above were classified as large, and those with employees less than 500 were classified as medium/small.

In order to be able to make statistically valid estimates simple random sampling design was adopted. Taking into account the specialized nature of the information to be collected, the relatively small number of food and agribusiness firms that have business interest in ESACs, and the survey being limited to firms in one country (UK), covering 1/4 of the working population, i.e. about 35 usable questionnaires, was taken as the target for the survey. At a response rate of 50%, questionnaires were mailed to 70 firms. To explain the reasons for the particular responses of executives, follow-up interviews were conducted with about 1/3 of the target respondents, i.e., with 12 executives. A total of 54 firms responded, giving response rate of 77%. The response rate considering only the usable questionnaires was 53%. The reasons why some firms did not complete the questionnaire were also compiled. Of the respondents of 37 firms, 19 were large firms, and 18 were medium/small firms.

In the questionnaire, the values were expressed on a dimension of agreement/disagreement, important/not important with the posited statement, on a 5 point scale in comparison to the listed variables, thus giving the data the ranking character. Therefore, as all tests involving the ranks of data are non-parametric, the non-parametric technique have been applied rather than the parametric techniques in analyzing the survey data.

Using the typology of statistical tests cited by Dillon et al. (1990) two tests, namely the Friedman test and the Mann-Whitney test were identified as appropriate for testing the null hypotheses. For tests involving the responses of the large and medium/small firm executives, where the two groups are independent, and the level of measurement ordinal, the Mann-Whitney test was used. For the test of hypotheses with regard the appropriateness/ importance of the various conditions, where the samples were more than three and related, and the level of measurement ordinal, the Friedman test was used.

Summary of major research findings and their implications

The study dealt with the three major determinants of JV formation in the agribusiness sector in SSACs: host country specific factors, foreign firm specific factors, and industry (the agribusiness) specific factors. The major findings corresponding these major determinants and their implications are summarized as follows.

Host country specific factors

The findings show that government policy, availability of capable host partners, size of national markets, shortage of foreign exchange, and distance between the center of major operations of the foreign firms and most SSACs are important factors that influence the decision of foreign firms to form a JV in SSACs.

Government policy: Evidence from the case study and review of policies of some SSACs revel that government policies are generally not conducive to JV entry by foreign firms for JV formation in the agribusiness sector. Few particular incentives or advantages provided for JVs were in evidence. Policy formulated were considered by respondents as often not clear, stable, nor properly implemented. Specific policy areas identified as generally unsatisfactory were: price regulations on inputs, company tax rates, profit and capital repatriation, ease of employing foreign staff, government incentives provided, lack of information on potential investment projects, lack of skilled manpower, and business ethics practiced.

Host partners: There is a scarcity of capable host private firms that meet the needs of foreign firms. Local firms differ in their capabilities to attract foreign firms as partners. The evidence from the case study lead to the classification of local agribusiness firms into 3 groups based on their capabilities for partnership with prospective foreign firms: readily capable partners, potentially capable partners, and incapable partners. Many firms, particularly in the medium/small category, have difficulty in searching for a partner, and lack the skill and other resources to prepare and propose investible projects to attract partners.

Host country market size: The limited size of national markets of most SSACs, both in terms of number of consumers and purchasing power has impeded the interest of foreign firms to form JVs.

Distance: The location of SSACs in relation to some of the investor countries, e.g. Japan, USA, UK and other European countries make venturing too expensive to the companies.

Major implications of these findings include the following:

i)   Most of the factors that foreign firms are not satisfied with are under government policy category which implied that they can be corrected with government action. To play a more effective role in the economy, JVs have to be promoted through implementing clear and supportive policies. Given the general preference for wholly owned subsidiaries (wos) by foreign firms, they have to be persuaded to prefer JVs. Discriminative tax incentives and profit repatriation could stimulate them more towards joint venturing. If no preference for JVs, then direct and indirect pressures on the foreign firms should not be exerted. However, business ethics, which is a part of the general socio-political and cultural setting, may not be tackled by government regulations alone. Its change is very much dependent on the progress of the political democratization, and economic liberalization which is taking place in many SSACs.

Lack of information on potential investment projects in SSACs implied that preparing and marketing investible projects would be an important strategy to attract foreign partners. Information and promotion should be marketing oriented, putting forward the advantage the foreign investor could attain in a JV, and how government and other concerned bodies will handle the various problems and obstacles that the foreign firm may face.

Lack of technical and managerial skill is found to be one of the major problems in SSACs. Paradoxically, unemployment including university and technical school graduates is also acute. This suggest that the training programs may not be tailored to the needs of industry. Therefore, among other steps, there appears to be a need of reexamining the educational and training policies and programs.

ii)   The reluctance of foreign firms to take state owned firms as partners on the one hand, and the general paucity of capable private firms on the other, calls for a strong program of support and promotion of the medium/small private firms. Such support can come from the national government, international organizations, and donor agencies. By making many host firms capable, foreign firms can have more choice and confidence in forming JVs. Thus, a JV formation model, involving a 'fourth link' is suggested that would be appropriate where there is a lack of readily capable host partners, but there are potentially capable host partners.

iii)   The small national markets of African countries have been identified among the serious constraints. Though establishing the African Economic Community, which has been on agenda since the 1960s and is still a long way off, strengthening regional markets through present arrangements - such as the Economic Community of West African States (ECOWAS), Southern Africa Development Co-ordinating Conference (SADCC), and Preferential Trade Area for Eastern and Southern African countries (PTA) allowing freer movement of goods cannot be overemphasized. This becomes more urgent in view of the small

174

size of current trade among African countries, estimated to be about 10% of their total trade. (M'baye 1992).

Encouraging inter-African trade is an important condition for attracting wider interest of foreign firms for joint venturing in particular and investment and trade in general. Though most countries have got a policy of self sufficiency in food, many are still dependent on imported food, thus food products give a wide opportunity for inter-African trade. The opportunities can be expected to be greater in the other sub-sector of agribusiness such as production and supply of farm machineries, fertilizers, chemicals, services, etc.

iv) Some evidences show that proximity and cultural similarity in the countries of respective partners have a strong influence in the formation of JVs. For example, of all JVs in China up to 1984, the foreign partners were from Hong Kong about 75% of the cases. Most of the investment in Poland come from West Germany (Beamish 1988). As outlined in Chapter 2, about 53% of partnerships including JVs recently formed in Western Europe were between partners within Western Europe, 36% with partners in Eastern Europe, and only the balance in other parts of the world. These evidences suggest that proximity to major sources of international investment plays an important role, which SSACs are in a disadvantage.

Because of distance, and the recent general disinterest by traditional investors mainly due to the problems of repatriation of profit and capital, and the limited national markets, governments and local firms in SSACs may increasingly be tempted to look for partners from other DCs, particularly Asian and Middle Eastern countries. Within Africa, the political development in the Republic of South Africa will have some positive impact particularly to southern and central African countries. South Africa, often grouped among the developed countries category, and with its advanced technology might be able to provide a new and additional impetus for investment. Similarly, North African countries (e.g. Egypt) can play similar role in their neighboring southern countries.

Foreign firm specific factors

The factors that were identified as firm specific determinants were the preferred market strategy of the firms, the preferred type of host partner, and the size of the particular firm.

Preferred strategy for business involvement: The findings showed that executives of foreign firms have different preferences among the alternative business participation forms in SSACs. Executives preferred wos, majority JVs and import/export compared to the other business participation forms. The least preferred forms were minority JVs and 50/50 JVs.

Preferred host partners for JV formation: Executives have also different preferences among the five types of host firms as suitable partners to form JVs. The order of suitability was: private firms, public companies, foreign firms, state-owned firms; and the least being cooperatives.

Large and medium/small foreign firms: One of the objectives of the study was to find out if there is any significant difference in the opinions and attitudes of executives of large foreign firms and medium/small foreign firms in terms of their preferences of market entry strategies, their preferences among host partners, the resources sought from host partners, and their evaluation of the host country specific JV entry environment.
The results are summarized as follows:

> -Both groups, executives of large firms and medium/small firms, were in agreement about the preferability/non-preferability of all forms except with regard wos and (foreign) majority JVs. Large firms were more inclined to involve in direct investment, i.e. in the modes of (foreign) majority JVs and wos, than medium/small firms.

> -Large firms and medium/small firms generally agree on the suitability/non-suitability of the different types of host partners for joint venturing.

> -There was no significant difference between the opinions of executives of large firms and medium/small firms with regard the importance of resources and attributes expected of the prospective host partners, and in their evaluation of host country specific JV

176

entry environment except in the case of 'business ethics'. A further examination of the data lead to the conclusion that medium/small firms find business ethical practices more problematic than their larger counterparts.

The findings have the following implications:

i)   Avoiding barriers on exercising management control and majority ownership by foreign firms is likely to enhance foreign investment in SSACs.

ii)   The strong preference for private firms and public companies and the low preference for state-owned firms and cooperatives imply that privatization would be a vehicle for attracting foreign firms in to partnership for JV in SSACs. This finding strengthens the need for recognizing the development of the private sector as central to the reform which African countries have embarked upon.

iii)   The need of resources in short supply in SSACs such as capital and technology is more likely to come from large firms rather than medium/small firms.

Agribusiness sector specific factors

As the basis for a JV is resource exchange between partners, the resources needed by foreign firms, and those needed and made available by prospective host partners in the agribusiness sector were examined. The results are summarized as follows:

i)   The most important resources and attributes sought by foreign firms were local influences/contacts, management/technical skills, marketing channels, financial contributions and access to agricultural land.

ii)   The major resources needed by local firms as contribution of the foreign partner were: export market access, improved technology (technical know-how and machinery) and new product ideas. The major resources and attributes the host partners are capable of contributing towards a JV were: internal market network, existing factory/business facilities, finance (local currency) and raw material supplies.

iii) Though there appeared to be a strong complementarity between the resources needed by the prospective foreign and host partners, a detailed examination revealed some discrepancies. The major ones were:

-As such attributes as local influence/contacts are intangible, there is a problem of determining their value in the capitalization process as a contribution of the host partner.

-Management/technical skills which foreign partners needed are not indicated among the resources made available by the host partners.

-Though marketing channels are required by foreign firms, and can be provided by the host partners, its effectiveness is undermined by the small size of the national markets.

These findings have the following implications:

i) Foreign firms are interested in the quality of the manpower (trained and skilled), rather than what may be termed as the quantity (untrained and unskilled) of labor. This finding strengthens the need of reviewing the manpower training policy in SSACs proposed previously.

ii) Foreign firms attach importance to the host partners financial contributions mainly to meet local cost (working capital), as this may account for a substantial portion of the whole capital outlay in the agri-production, processing and marketing process. Access to credit with favorable terms to the host partner could strengthen his position.

iii) Privatization of land, and provision for long term land concession for direct foreign investment is likely to attract more foreign firms in the agribusiness sector of SSACs. Privatization would reduce the consideration of intangible attributes by foreign firms, and would strengthen the position of the host partner. However, this strategy has to be carefully worked out so as settled communities are not displaced.

iv) Generally, the resources made available by host partners in agribusiness lack uniqueness, placing them in a weaker position. Owing to this, host partners are likely to accept a minority position in a JV. Various training and advice to prospective partners to specialize is also important to make the host firm a more capable partner.

Conclusion and recommendations

Conclusion

The findings of this study show that some of the determining factors for JV formation in the agribusiness sector in SSACs can be positively influenced by policies of the respective governments of these countries, while some others must be tackled by a coordinated action on regional and international level.

During the last three years more than 35 African countries have moved towards political pluralism and democracy. Economic liberalization and privatization is likely to create a much better environment for JV formation. The reforms will help narrow the gap between policies formulated and their implementation, which were among the basic constraints for inflow of foreign investment in general and JV formation in particular. However, the situation must be viewed in the context of the burden of external debt estimated at $271.1 billion in 1991 (M'baye), and the drought problem which have aggravated the economic ills of SSACs.

The policy reforms underway need substantial support from donor countries and international organizations not only in terms of development assistance, but also in finding a way out of the debt crisis. Such support is necessary if privatization, market integration and the development of capital markets is to succeed. Only through such concerted national, regional and international efforts can joint venturing in the agribusiness sector of SSACs rapidly grow with considerable impact on economic development. Therefore, from the findings of this research two sets of recommendations, i.e., for host country governments, and for developed country governments and international organizations are proposed. The major international organizations referred to here are the World Bank,

179

OECD, IMF, and pertinent UN organizations such as UNIDO, UNDP and FAO.

The assumptions made in recommending courses of action for the developed country governments and international organizations are:

-There is a desire by developed country governments and international organizations to rethink and reassess materially their various aid programs to SSACs;

-The debt problem and other environmental issues such as the drought affecting a large section of SSACs call for a global solution;

-The development aid program provided to DCs from the developed countries averaged about 0.33% of their GNP (Montagnon 1990), and there is a wide room to raise this percentage substantially;

-The ebb of the cold war, and therefore the ease in the armament race could release substantial financial and scientific resources that could be diverted to development aid programs;

-Sub-Saharan Africa is the most needy of development assistance among the regions of the world, and developed countries will find it appropriate to formulate partial arrangements for the region; and

-In the long run, the impact of the development assistance, i.e., the creation of wider and richer markets would be of mutual benefit.

Recommendations for host country governments

i)   To formulate a more discriminative incentives for JVs and partners through taxes, profit repatriation, and access to credit.

ii)   To allow ownership and management control strictly at par with contributions of the host and foreign partners with out conditions of host majority ownership and control of the venture.

iii)   To recognize the development of the private sector as central to economic development of the country. This requires building the confidence and status of the country's private sector through

180

privatizing the agro-processing and marketing sector thereby creating more capable host private sector partners.

iv) To employ resources, recovered by way of privatization to improve the infrastructure, provide agricultural inputs and extension programs, and training to the rural sector, whose raised income and active participation in the market is an important condition for growth of JVs.

v) To support particularly medium/small firms:

-In preparing their JV project proposals;

-In collecting and providing information about prospective foreign partners;

-By providing partial/full travel expenses for foreign visits to negotiate for JVs; and,

-By providing concessionary loans.

vi) To strengthen various private sector associations such as chambers of commerce, farmers associations, cooperatives, trade associations through financial and material resources, and training so that they become more capable of providing essential services to their respective members.

vii) To accelerate the integration of African regional markets to create a wider and more sustainable opportunity for JVs, and other companies whose operations might have been undermined by small national markets.

viii) To review the manpower training programs so that they are tailored to serve the specific requirements of the various sectors of the economy.

ix) To review the employment policy in a way to attract able and qualified foreign skills, as well as wooing professional nationals who, due to unfavorable home employment conditions are working elsewhere outside of the region.

x)   To decontrol prices of agro-processing inputs which can encourage price differentiation and increased production of those produces that the agro-processing sector requires.

Recommendations for developed country governments and international organizations

i)   To support the JV formation process by participating as a catalyst partner (i.e. as the fourth link in the proposed model). Specific courses of action include:

-Participate in JVs by contributing resources the host partner is unable to provide, particularly foreign currency;

-Provide guarantee for the acquisition of machinery and equipment, if the JV requires importation of such machinery;

-Provide guarantee for the profit repatriation of the foreign partner through its injection of foreign currency.

ii)   To provide special preferential arrangements for agro-processed products from SSACs.

iii)   To strengthen by training and material support the basic organizations of the private sector such as chambers of commerce, confederations of industries, trade associations and cooperatives so that they are able to reach the small entrepreneur across the country.

iv)   To support the market integration programs of the countries of the region through provision of infrastructural, financial and organizational resources.

v)   To assist in overcoming the debt burden of SSACs.

Contributions of the study

This study claims a number of contributions which can be grouped into theoretical, methodological and empirical.

Theoretical contributions

i)   Relatively little work has been done on less developed countries in general, and in countries of sub-Saharan Africa in particular with regard to the role of JVs.

ii)   Previous studies of JVs covered the manufacturing sector generally, without due consideration of the particular characteristics of the agribusiness sector.

iii)   Though partner needs and selection is often identified as the most important factor in the formation and success of JVs, the level of attention given to it in JV literature has been relatively inadequate. This study dealt with the attitudes and capabilities of both the foreign and host partners, thereby identifying how better the needs of the respective partners could be met.

iv)   Previous literature of JVs described foreign partners from developed countries as MNCs (or TNCs) with little attempt to examine if there are any differences among them in their attitudes towards JV formation particularly in DCs. This study examined the attitudes of foreign firms by distinguishing between 'large firms' and 'medium/small firms'.

This study has contributed towards filling the gap that existed in the JV literature with regard to these important issues.

Methodological contributions

i)   The survey approach has been the most commonly used method in studies of JVs. The application of the case study approach has been limited, mainly because the method is generally perceived to be not suitable for rigorous analysis. Some authors, notably Yin (1989) and Smith (1990) proposed that the case study method is as sound as any other method provided appropriate procedures and analytical

183

techniques are applied. In this study, the case study method has been used with the recommended procedures and analytical techniques and useful conclusions and theories have been generated.

ii) Among the problems faced in attempting to survey UK based agribusiness firms with business interests in Africa has been the lack of a list that can serve as a sampling frame. Therefore, a list of such firms has been compiled by referring to various sources over the period extending almost the duration of the research. A data-base of UK based food and agribusiness firms with business interests in ESACs is now available. With further updating, it can be a basis for future research in the area.

Empirical contributions

Through the analysis of the host-country specific JV entry environment, the study has examined the major barriers, some opportunities for JV formation, and has shown how JVs can be promoted in the agribusiness sector of SSACs, an area of high priority for development. The classification of local firms on a criterion of their capability as prospective host partners is the first attempt in the JV literature. Though the classification need be refined from situations and experiences from other SSACs, it however enabled the direction of policy and assistance that are appropriate for local firms. A model where foreign institutions and governments can involve into the JV promotion in a SSACs is proposed.

The survey of UK based agribusiness firms has identified the conditions that would encourage them to enter JVs in SSACs. This will help in formulating policy by SSACs with a more market oriented approach, i.e., with a view of satisfying the needs of the foreign investor.

Some limitations of the study

i) The study was concerned with a sub-sector of agribusiness, i.e., the production, processing and marketing of food and drinks products. It did not cover the input sub-sector, production and supply of implements and other farm machineries, fertilizers, seeds, pesticides, etc.

ii) Agribusiness is closely related to the land tenure system, and the organization of agricultural production. The study did not address this issue as it was beyond the scope defined for the study.

iii) The respondents to the questionnaire gave their opinions and attitudes with regard to joint venturing in the ESACs. From the results generalizations to SSACs have been made. While most characteristics can justify their common treatment, the effects of regional and cultural diversities like the Francophone West African countries, Portuguese speaking countries, and regional associations such as ECOWAS, PTA, SADCC was not considered in the study.

iv) As this study is basically exploratory, the medium/small category of firms were defined very broadly, i.e., with employees of less than 500. For instance, the medium/small category was found to be too broad including small firms with a few employees and engaged only in operations of limited scope (such as import or export only) on the one hand, and medium firms with relatively abundant manpower, capital resources with diversified activities in African countries and other regions on the other.

v) The strength in focusing on UK based agribusiness firms was that it would allow a more thorough examination of the problem (such as through face-to-face personal interviews) resulting in more practical recommendations. However, this is also a limitation. Generalizations made to 'foreign firms' based on these findings may raise some questions, as some sources (e.g. Hill 1981, Franko 1987) indicate that investors of various origins (such as US, UK, Japan, continental Europe) may differ in their attitudes towards participating in JVs.

A pointer for further research

i) A similar study of determinants of JV formation in the other subsectors of agribusiness, i.e., the input industries (production and marketing of farm machineries and implements, fertilizers, pesticides, etc.) would be very useful, and could complement the findings of this study to give a more complete understanding of the JV formation environment in the agribusiness sector of SSACs.

ii)   The impact of land ownership and the organization of agricultural production on the types of prospective host partners, and the foreign firms participation in JVs is another area where further research can focus.

iii)   Though SSACs have common development problems to surmount, it would be misleading to assume that they can always be considered in same manner. Countries differ in their national characteristics which impact on business culture, policy, and above all in their resource endowments. Therefore, detailed investigations of country and region specific opportunities and policies to promote JVs in the agribusiness sector are necessary.

iv)   The assumption in favor of medium/small foreign firms were: small firms are relatively labor oriented, and therefore generate more employment; medium/small foreign firms can be regarded as more 'equal partners' with the firms in African countries than the big multinationals; they can be interested and satisfied with African markets which might be considered too small by large firms; and they may be more in need of the host partner than the large firms.

The findings of this study showed that there is very little difference between the attitudes of large and medium/small firms. However, the result might have been affected by the criterion chosen to classify large and medium/small firms which did not fully account for their differing characteristics. A more refined classification of firms would enable to design specific policies both for the home and host countries for promoting investments in general and joint venturing in particular.

v)   Investors may differ in their propensity to go into JVs. For instance, US and UK companies are said to be more reluctant to go into JVs than companies of other origin, like Japan, continental Europe and emerging DCs (India, South Korea, Brazil, China, etc.). Comparative studies with regard to these sources of partners for JVs in the agribusiness sector will broaden the opportunities for acquiring the required resources needed by SSACs.

vi)   In analyzing the changes in the food processing industry in Europe, McGee and Segal-Horn (1988) indicated that the industry has passed through a number of phases: a period of whole-sale dominations (the 1930s), manufacturers dominations (1960s), the rise of the retailers (1970s), and 'the era in which the consumer is expected to be king' (current). The last phase has also been commonly described in the marketing literature as 'marketing orientation' of the mission, strategies and objectives of firms to satisfy their customers. The response to and the impact of these developments on the agribusiness production and marketing system in general, and the extent of the major retailers involvement in JVs and other business types with firms in African countries in particular need be thoroughly investigated. For instance, Sainsbury introduced about 1,500 new items to their shelves in 1991 alone (Hosking 1992), among which are food and drinks products. To study what proportion of these products originate from SSACs, whether these have been declining or increasing, and what can be done to increase the shelve space for African products with the cooperation of the retailers possibly by way of JVs is important considering the priority given for agro-based exports by African countries. This can be viewed in the context of the wider market of the European Union.

References

Beamish, P.W.(1988). *Multinational Joint Ventures in Developing Countries*. London: Routledge.

Chen, E.K.Y.(ed.) (1990). *Foreign Direct Investment in Asia*. Tokyo: Asia productivity Organization.

Dillon, W.R. et al.(1990). *Marketing Research in a Marketing Environment*. 2nd edition. Boston: Richard D Irwin, Inc.

Franko, L.G.(1987). 'New Forms of Investment in Developing Countries by US Companies: a Five Industries Comparison', *The Columbia Journal of World Business*. vol.22 no.2 pp.39-55.

Hill, R.(1981). 'Are Multinationals Aliens in the Third World?', *International Management*. January. pp.12-16.

Hosking, P.(1992). 'Sainsbury Profits from New Lines', *The Independent*. May 14. p.1.

M'baye, S.(1992). 'Rebuilding the Continent', *West Africa.* May 11-17. pp.797-798.

McGee, J. & Segal-Horn, S.(1989). 'Changes in the European Food Processing Industry: the Consequences of 1992', *Working Paper SWP 29/89.* Cranfield: Cranfield School of Management.

Montagnon, P.(1990). 'The Good and Bad News for Aid Recipients', *Financial Time.* December 6. p.2.

Smith, N.C.(1990). 'The Case Study: A Vital Yet Misunderstood Research Method for Management', *Graduate Management Research.* vol.4 no.4 pp.4-26.

Yin, R.K.(1989). *Case Study Research: Design and Methods.* Applied social research methods series. vol.5. Newbury Park: SAGE Publications Inc.

Appendices

Jos International Breweries Ltd. (Nigeria)

Summary profile: Partners: local government 50%, A/S Cerekem (Danish) 12.5%, 'Industrialization Fund for DCs' (Denmark) 12.5%, and other investors (unspecified) 25%. Established in 1979; JV managed by Cerekem. Since its formation, the JV has developed into one of the most advanced integrated agricultural enterprises in Nigeria, with several subsidiaries of its own.

Benefits to the host partners: employment generation: about 1,600 people; revenue from excise & corporate income; diversification: (besides brewery, crop production, milling, poultry, cattle & pig production, etc.); use of local raw materials, & import substitution thereby contributing towards the self-sufficiency objective; extensive research program in crop production & processing; new product development. (e.g. corn flakes, syrups, etc.).

Benefits to the foreign partners: substantial dividends earned; sales of know-how & machinery; fulfillment of strategic objectives.

Reasons for success: a large & growing market for beer; and management & know-how of the foreign partner.

Olivine (Zimbabwe)

Summary profile: Partners: Zimbabwe government (49%) and Heinz Co. (51%). JV formed in 1982. Major products include cooking oil, margarine, soaps, canned vegetables, etc. The company is growing fast; by 1986 annual sales exceeded $80 million, and exports grew from $1 million to $15 million.

Benefits to the host partner: employment generation: 1,500 people; growing foreign exchange from exports; local management of the venture; new technology and skills; revenue from tax; partner assistance in other areas: (improved seed, technology and extension work in agriculture & food production).

Benefits to the foreign partner: majority ownership (51%); technical control; entry to Zimbabwe, & consequently to the regional market; satisfactory rate of return on investment.

Reasons for success: high commitment from the foreign partner; pragmatism and compromises from both sides; selection of competent management.

Mumias Sugar Company

Summary profile: Partners: Kenya government (71%), East African Development Bank (2.6%), Kenya Commercial Finance (5%), CDC (17%), and Booker McConnell (4.4%). Formed in 1971, after thorough feasibility study between 1960-1970. 12% of cane produced by the Company's 'nucleus estate', while the bulk (88%) supplied by the 'out-growers' numbering about 23,000. The company supplies about 50% of the domestic consumption of sugar.

Benefits to the host partners: significant contribution to the import substitution objective; cash economy to a relatively poor region; employment (5,000 permanent & 9,000 seasonal); technological dissemination: improved agricultural production; emergence of local entrepreneurship; government revenues from taxes, and overall development: urbanization, schools, medical, and other institutions and infrastructure affecting about 350,000 people.

Benefits to the foreign partners: high international reputation for the successful management of the project; satisfactory return on equity and management fees; control of the venture through contract management.

Reasons for success: Government of Kenya's positive attitudes towards commercial agriculture, its pragmatism and flexibility; favorable loans from financiers; land use system where cane as well as food crops are grown by the farmers (accompanied with improved technology and supervision).

Kenyan Tea Development Authority (KTDA)

Summary profile: Partners: Kenyan Government, farmers, & CDC. The Company is a production-processing-marketing enterprise for tea; the largest exporter of black tea in the world; organized about 138,000 small holders to plant about 54,000 ha.

Benefits to the host partners: foreign exchange (85% of production is for export); technology dissemination (techniques of growing, packing, processing and marketing tea to a wider area involving small-holders); and government revenues from taxes.

Benefits to the foreign partners: the organization has slowly transformed into a local entity recently, and foreign participation is in the form of extending credit (World Bank, OPEC, USAID); and as such no direct benefit except interest is recorded.

Reasons for success: non-interference by government in the enterprise's operations; management system that ensures reward for high performance; and efficient system for quality control.

Note

The above cases were compiled from the following sources: the Courier no.102 March/April 1987, Dibb 1987, O'Reilly 1988, Robbs 1989, Abbott 1987, George 1977, William & Karen 1985, William & Karen 1985.

191

Appendix B

The case study protocol (A pan for conducting a case study of the JV formation environment in the agribusiness sector in Zimbabwe)

Overview

Background

One observation from the JV literature review is the general lack of information with regard to African countries. Tackling the research problem identified for the study required documentation and analysis of the JV environment in the African country setting. The alternative methods commonly used for collecting data are surveying and case study. The argument for using the case study approach, the reasons for selecting Zimbabwe for the case were discussed in Chapter 4. This case study protocol is a detail plan for collecting data in Zimbabwe.

Purpose

i)   To explore the entry environment for foreign firms to form JVs in the food and agribusiness sector in Zimbabwe, particularly in terms of government policy, and availability of capable host partners;

ii)   To indicate areas of JV opportunities in the food and agribusiness sector in Zimbabwe; and

iii)   To identify major barriers that inhibit JV formation in the food and agribusiness sector of Zimbabwe.

The research question and propositions

The research question: The research question for the case study is: how conducive is the JV entry environment for foreign firms in the food and agribusiness sector of Zimbabwe? If conducive, what are the strengths? If not conducive, what are the major barriers, and how can they be overcome? The question deals with two major factors:

192

i) Government policy: Does the Zimbabwe government promote JVs in the agribusiness sector of the economy, and if so, how effective has it been in attracting foreign partners?

ii) Availability of capable host partners: Who are the potential host partners; what are their strengths and weaknesses; do they opt for JVs, and why?

Theoretical propositions: The following theoretical Propositions were generated in order to analysis the data, match the various evidences, and arrive at conclusions. The propositions are based on the discussions given in Chapter 2, particularly the section dealing with why governments of DCs favor JVs. The propositions are stated as follows:

i) Government policy: Lacking many critical resources for their development programs, DCs depend on external sources to acquire these resources. As a balancing mechanism in meeting the objectives of acquiring these resources and control over their economies they find joint venturing an attractive option. It is proposed that, therefore, these objectives are expressed as policies, and that strategies to promote JVs in terms of incentives and other supports are made available to JVs and/or to the partners. JVs established have benefited from such incentives and supports, and companies are expecting these benefits.

ii) Host partners: One of the major determinants of JV formation in DCs is the availability of capable partners in the host country. Host partners have different existing or potential strengths and weaknesses in resource allocation depending on their nature of organization and ownership structure. It is expected that local firms with ample resources are scarce and there is a need to promote the less capable ones with various supports.

Prospective host firms will look for foreign partners rather than Zimbabwean firms as partners. This is mainly for two reasons: a) the resources they seek from partners are not available within Zimbabwe, b) they aspire to inter the export market which is better accessed through foreign firms.

JV formation in DCs is generally preceded by other looser modes of business relations between the host firm and the foreign firm, such as import/export, agency, contract agreements, purchase/sales agreements, etc. It is proposed that partners of JVs already set up had such looser business relationships and present local firms in import/export, agency, etc. aspire for turning their relations into JVs. It is expected that JVs operating have resulted from previous involvements of the partners in business relations, and host companies aspiring for JVs have got business relations with the prospective foreign firm(s).

Organization of the plan

This plan is organized into 4 sections. The overview section outlines the background of the case study of Zimbabwe, the purpose of the study, and the research question and propositions. Section 2 discusses the preparations to be made by the researcher for the successful completion of the field work in Zimbabwe. Section 3 comprises 4 sets of case study questions, each aimed at different respondents interested or involved in policy formulation, implementation, promotion and operation of JVs particularly in the agribusiness sector of Zimbabwe. In the last section, an outline that will guide the write-up of the final case study report is proposed.

Field procedures

Preparations

The preparation aspect comprises of securing sufficient financial support, the necessary travel documents, working materials such as print outs of the case study questions, diskettes, lists and addresses of contacts, a working and staying places in Harare, and an introduction letter.

The researcher has ensured that all the above were available prior to the field trip. As contacts in Zimbabwe were crucial, considerable effort was made to identify knowledgeable persons as advisers and informants during the conduct of the field work. Over the preparation period, two persons in the University of Zimbabwe, two executives of two private firms, an official of an international organizations (FAO), all based in Harare, the capital of Zimbabwe, were identified and letters sent to them about the program of the field work, and the possible area of their support.

The field work was scheduled to take a maximum of 10 weeks, from 12 August 1991 to 31 October 1991. However, the program of work is planned for a period of 8 weeks, leaving the remaining 2 weeks for unexpected situations that may elongate the field work.

Potential sources of data

From the desk study, some potential sources of data were identified, including the following:

Organizations:

i)   Pertinent government organizations (Zimbabwe Investment Center, Zimbabwe National Bank, etc.)

ii)   JV senior management (Olivine, etc.)

iii)   JV partners (CDC, etc.)

iv)   Branch offices of international organizations (UNDP, FAO, PTA, etc.)

v)   Private firms (EDESA Ltd., MBB Pvt. Ltd., etc.)

vi)   Confederation of Zimbabwe Industries (CZI)

vii)   Zimbabwe National Chamber of Commerce (ZNCC)

viii)   Foreign trade missions in Harare (UK, USA, Japan, etc.)

ix)   The University of Zimbabwe

Documents:

i)   Investment laws and regulations of Zimbabwe

ii)   Periodicals and newspapers

iii)   National Bank reports

iv)   Annual reports (of relevant companies)

v)   Annual statistical reports (national)

The plan is to contact, as soon as possible, the individuals who pledged support, and with them to identify other interviewees. A 'snow-balling' technique will be used to reach the pertinent people that can provide the required data.

Case study questions

Various types of respondents that have interest in promoting or establishing JVs in Zimbabwe were targeted for data collection. The following are the different forms designed to be used in each case.

Form B.1(1)
Opinions and attitudes of executives about JV formation environment in Zimbabwe

Name of the JV

Partners: a) Host
              b) Foreign

Name of interviewee
Position of interviewee

1. Government support at the beginning
        -Incentives
                -Locational
                -Tax holiday
                -Financial
        -Project approval
        -Supporting offices
        -Other

2. Previous relation with the partner

-Importing from
-Exporting to
-Technical agreements
-Managerial agreements
-Financial relations
-Hire/purchase agreements
-Agency
-No previous relations

3. Contributions of host partner

-Technical know-how
-Managerial know-how
-Improved technology
-Machinery
-Financial
    -foreign exchange
    -local
-Internal market network
-Factory facilities
-Agri-land
-Office building
-Local contacts
-Raw materials supplies

4. Contributions of foreign partner

-Technical know-how
-Management know-how
-Improved technology
-Machinery
-Foreign exchange
-Local
-Export market
-New product ideas

5. Level of host ownership

-More than 50%

-Coownership (50-50%)
-Less than 50%

6. Current problems

    -Financial
    -Raw material
    -Technical
    -Marketing
    -Managerial

7. On the whole, satisfied with the JV?

Form B.2
Opinions and attitudes of officials of investment promotion organizations about JV formation environment in Zimbabwe

Name of the organization
Name of interviewee
Position of interviewee

1. Does government policy encourage JVs compared to other forms?

2. What are government supports for JVs?

    -Incentives
      -Locational
      -Tax holiday
      -Financial
      -Profit repatriations
      -Other

    -Project approval

    -Supporting offices

3. General comments

Form B.3
Opinions and attitudes of officials of foreign trade missions about JV formation environment in Zimbabwe

Trade mission for (name of country)
Name of interviewee
Position of interviewee

1. Does government policy encourage JVs compared to other forms?

2. How do they evaluate the business environment for companies from their respective countries to go into JVs? (good, not good)

3. How would they evaluate the following as a problem for foreign businesses? (big, somewhat, not so much)

   -Bureaucracy
   -Threats of nationalization
   Capital & profit repatriation

4. General comments

Form B.4
Opinions and attitudes of local small businesses seeking JV partners

1. What are the key aspects of your business?

   -Name of the company
   -Year established

   -Type of ownership (please mark as appropriate)

   -private   -partnership
   -cooperative   -public company
   -other (please specify)

   -Nature of the business (a brief note on activities of the company)

199

2. Is a JV partnership desired by your company?

    -Yes   -No

3. Please state your reasons for the above reply:

4. What would be the contributions of your company towards the JV? (e.g. buildings, land, cash, existing business facilities, etc.) Please list below.

5. Do you think you will find your future partner within Zimbabwe ?

    -Yes   -No

6. What organizational form would the JV take?

    -To establish a new and separate company

    -To improve/expand the existing facility

    -Other

7. What is the percentage share desired by your company in the JV?

    -Equal share (on 50/50 basis)

    -Majority share for your company (>50%)

    -Minority share for your company (<50%)

    -Negotiable

8. Have you obtained any support in your effort to find a partner?

    -Yes   -No

9. If yes, which organization rendered which kind of support?

Organization	Kind of support
a)	1)
b)	2)
c)	3)

Guide for the case study report

1. Introduction

2. A brief description of the business environment in Zimbabwe (from secondary data)

3. A summary of interview data on government policy, capability of host partners, and attitudes about JVs

4. A review of theoretical propositions posited at the beginning of the case study

5. Major findings and conclusions

6. List of organizations visited for interview.

Notes

1. While Form B.1 was the standard questionnaire used for gathering data from agribusiness enterprises, some items have been changed slightly to fit the characteristics of 3 types of respondents: executives of operating JVs, executives of firms that are in the process of forming JVs, and those that showed the interest and intention of forming JVs.

Questionnaire: A survey of the attitudes of senior executives of UK food and agribusiness companies about JV formation in African countries

Note:

For the purpose of this study:

1. A *joint venture* refers to a business collaboration undertaken between a UK based firm (the foreign partner), and one or more firm(s) in an African country (the host partner/s), for their mutual benefit. The UK firm may contribute such resources as machineries and equipment, technology, management and technical know-how, export market access, etc.; while the host firm(s) may contribute local resources such as land, buildings, local currency, market channels, raw materials, local management, etc.

2. *Africa*: refers to *English-speaking Africa* (see map).

Question 1

During an exploratory survey for this study, UK executives were asked what were their business strategies for entering and expanding in markets of DCs. They mentioned several, which could be categorized as shown below. With regard to the African countries, how would you evaluate each option listed below in achieving your company's objectives? Please circle one number for each strategy. 5 means *most appropriate* and 1 means *not appropriate at all*.

Establishing a wholly owned subsidiary of your Co.   5   4   3   2   1

Establishing a majority JV (your Co.'s share >50%)   5   4   3   2   1

Establishing a co-owned (50-50%) JV   5   4   3   2   1

Establishing a minority JV (your Co.'s share <50%)   5   4   3   2   1

Through management/technical agreements	5	4	3	2	1
Through licensing agreements	5	4	3	2	1
Through direct export/import only	5	4	3	2	1

Question 2

Generally, UK companies wishing to establish joint ventures in the African countries may form them in partnership with one of the following types of firms.
How would you evaluate each one as a suitable host partner?
Please circle one number for each type. 5 means *most suitable*, and 1 means *not suitable at all*.

Private sector firms	5	4	3	2	1
Public sector (state-owned) firms	5	4	3	2	1
Co-operatives	5	4	3	2	1
Public companies (share companies)	5	4	3	2	1
Foreign firms in the host country	5	4	3	2	1
Others (please specify)	5	4	3	2	1

_____

_____

Question 3

Has your organization formed a joint venture(s) in any of the African countries?

Yes __   How many?   __ 1
                                 __ 2-3
                                 __ 4 or more

Not yet, but we are considering possibilities ___

No, we do not find joint ventures appropriate ___

Question 4

If your answer to question 3 above is yes, which of the following best represents your experience of joint ventures in Africa?

All/most are satisfactory ___

Some are, others are not satisfactory ___

None/very few are satisfactory ___

Question 5

In considering forming a joint venture in an African country what are the attributes you seek from your host partner(s)? Please circle one number per statement. 5 means *most important* and 1 means *not important at all*.

Financial contributions	5	4	3	2	1
Management/technical skills	5	4	3	2	1
Marketing channels	5	4	3	2	1
Local influence/contacts	5	4	3	2	1
Local technology	5	4	3	2	1
Machinery & equipment	5	4	3	2	1
Offices and buildings	5	4	3	2	1
Cheap labor	5	4	3	2	1
Supply of raw materials	5	4	3	2	1

| Access to agricultural land | 5 | 4 | 3 | 2 | 1 |

| Others: please specify | 5 | 4 | 3 | 2 | 1 |

_____

_____

Question 6

Establishing a joint venture might be a difficult undertaking for various reasons. During an exploratory survey for this study, UK executives interviewed have mentioned 23 factors that influence their decisions whether to form a joint venture or not. Taking in to consideration your most recent experience, to what extent each of the following factors has been seen as an important factor to your company in deciding to form or not to form a joint venture in an African country?

Please circle one number per statement on the scale:

4 indicates that you found the particular situation in the host country to be *very satisfactory*

3 indicates to be just *satisfactory*

0 indicates that it was *not applicable*

2 indicates that the particular situation in the host country was *unsatisfactory*

1 indicates that the particular situation in the host country was *prohibitively unsatisfactory.*

| The application & approval process of establishing a JV | 4 | 3 | 2 | 1 | 0 |

| Ease of importations of raw materials & parts | 4 | 3 | 2 | 1 | 0 |

| Domestic raw materials supplies | 4 | 3 | 2 | 1 | 0 |

| Price regulations on inputs | 4 | 3 | 2 | 1 | 0 |

Price regulations on final products	4	3	2	1	0
Ease of employing foreign staff	4	3	2	1	0
Availability of capable host partners	4	3	2	1	0
Availability of management skills	4	3	2	1	0
Protection from nationalization	4	3	2	1	0
Profit and capital repatriation	4	3	2	1	0
Banking & financial facilities	4	3	2	1	0
Efficiencies in executing business operations	4	3	2	1	0
Host country market size and prospect of expansion	4	3	2	1	0
Availability of skilled manpower	4	3	2	1	0
Availability of cheap labor	4	3	2	1	0
Availability of information on potential projects	4	3	2	1	0
Business ethics (absence of bribes, nepotism, etc.)	4	3	2	1	0
Government incentives provided (eg. tax concessions, grants, loans, etc.)	4	3	2	1	0
Company tax rates	4	3	2	1	0
Political situation (peaceful & stable environment)	4	3	2	1	0
Work ethics (workers discipline, productivity, etc)	4	3	2	1	0
Infrastructure (e.g. ports, transport, telephone, etc.)	4	3	2	1	0
Regulations on management-employee relations	4	3	2	1	0

Question 7

For how long has your organization been active in Africa?

<5 years ____   5-10 years ____   > 10 years ____

Question 8

During the period you have been active in Africa, which of the following business operations were you engaged in? Please tick as appropriate.

	Yes	No
Wholly owned manufacturing interests	--	--
Joint manufacturing/processing ventures	--	--
Contract farming	--	--
Licensing agreements	--	--
Management/technical services	--	--
Exporting to African countries	--	--
Importing from African countries	--	--
Other please specify	--	--

_____

_____

Thank you for your consideration and help.

Appendix D

Interview guide for the pilot study

Introduction

The researcher starts by briefly outlining the objectives of the study and methodology employed, indicating the importance of the findings both to UK based agribusiness companies and similar companies in Africa for promoting their business relationships. Then, the following points are raised by the researcher for discussion with the particular executive of the company.

Company objectives and strategies

1.   International business participation forms employed by the company in SSACs

2.   Whether there is a preference to a specific type(s) of business participation forms in SSACs

3.   If there is, which and why?

4.   The major objectives they set out to attain from their business participation in SSACs

     -For the company

     -For the host country

Host partners

1.   The type of host partners they have experienced with in SSACs (privately owned firms, state-owned firms, foreign firms, others)

208

2. Whether there is a preference by the company among the types of partners mentioned to form a JV in SSACs

3. If there is, which and why?

JV experience

1. How is a JV differentiated from other business participation forms?

2. The level of ownership and management control wanted by the company in a JV in SSACs

3. The major host-country specific entry barriers into a JV in SSACs.

4. Details of some JVs of the company in SSACs: (if possible collection of supporting materials)

5. The possibility of taking one of the company's JV in a SSAC for a case study during the field work in African countries

Any comments and suggestions by the interviewee

Appendix E

Follow-up interview schedule to supplement the questionnaire survey

Company name

In reference to question 1: (Opinions on the international business participation forms as a strategy for achieving company objectives);

Observe the pattern of reply and ask: Why are some of the options considered more appropriate and other are not?

In reference to question 2: (Opinions and attitudes with regard to suitability of the different host partners);

Observe the pattern of reply and ask: Why are some types of partners considered more suitable than others?

In reference to question 3: (Experience with JVs);

If the reply is yes, they have JVs, then ask:

-In which African country(ies) are the JVs?

-Whether they are successful or unsuccessful?

If the reply is not currently but they have intentions for the future, then ask:

-The stage of the study/formation process at present

-Problems faced

If the reply is no, they do not have JVs currently and do not intend to form one in the future, then ask: Why?

In reference to question 4: (Degree of satisfaction with the JVs they have got);

Regarding those which are satisfactory, why were they considered satisfactory?

Regarding those which are not satisfactory, why were they considered unsatisfactory?

In reference to question 5: (Most important resources and attributes sought from prospective host partners);

Observe pattern of reply and then ask: Why are some considered important while others not?

In reference to question 6: (Evaluation of host-country specific factors in the JV formation decision);

Observe and identify factors falling on the extremes of the scale and find out the reasons:

Bibliography

Abbott, J.C.(1988). *Agricultural Processing for Development*. Aldershot: Gower Publishing Co. Ltd.

_____, (1987). *Agricultural Marketing Enterprises in Developing Countries*. Cambridge: Cambridge University Press.

ADA (1991). *ADA: Annual Report and Accounts, 1989/90*. Harare.

AEA (the Agricultural Engineers Association), *Overseas Information Bulletin*, Week 37, 14 September 1990.

Afriyie, K.(1988). 'Factor Choice Characteristics and Industrial Impact of Joint Ventures: Lessons From a Developing Economy', *Columbia Journal of World Business*. vol.23 no.2. pp.51-61.

Agodo, O. (1978). 'The Determinants of US Private Manufacturing Investments in Africa', *Journal of International Business*. vol.10. Winter. pp.95-107.

Akinsanya, A.A.(1989). 'Economic Nationalism in Africa: Illusion and Reality', *TransAfrica Forum*. vol.6 no.2. pp.49-60.

Amador R.E. & Starbird, S.A.(1989). 'The Evaluation of International Agribusiness Investment Locations Using Multidimensional Scaling', *Agribusiness*. vol.5 no.2. pp.139-51.

Artisien, P.F.R.(1985). *Joint Ventures in Yugoslav Industry*. Gower Publishing Co. Ltd.

Auster, E.R.(1987). 'International Corporate Linkages: Dynamic Forms in Changing Environments', *The Columbia Journal of World Business*. vol.22 no.2. pp.3-6.

Babbie, E.R.(1973). *Survey Research Methods*. Belmont: Wadsworth Publishing Co. Inc.

Barabba, V.P.(1990). 'The Marketing Research Encyclopedia', *Harvard Business Review*. January/February.

Barry, F.(1991). 'Industrialisation Strategies for Developing Countries: Lessons from the Irish Experience', *Development Policy Review*. vol.9 no.1 pp.85-98.

Batezat, E. et al.(1986). 'The Working Conditions of Female Workers in the Food Processing Industry in Zimbabwe (with special reference to canneries)', *Working Papers No.10*. Harare: Zimbabwe Institute of Development Studies.

Baum, W.C. & Tolbert, S.M. (1985). *Investing in Development: Lessons of World Bank Experience*. New York: Oxford University Press.

Beamish, P.W.(1988). *Multinational Joint Ventures in Developing Countries*. London: Routledge.

_____, (1987). 'Joint Ventures in Less Developed Countries: Partner Selection & Performance', *Management International Review*. vol.27 no.1. pp.23-37.

_____, (1985). 'The Characteristics of Joint Ventures in Developed and Developing Countries', *Columbia Journal of World Business*. vol.20 no.3. pp.13-19.

Bennell, P.(1990). 'British Industrial Investment in Sub-Saharan Africa: Corporate Responses to Economic Crisis in the 1980s', *Development Policy Review*. vol.8 no.2. pp.155-77.

Bennett, R.(1986). 'Meaning and Method in Management Research', *Graduate Management Research*. Special Issue. Vol.3 No.3. pp.4-56.

Best of British: the Top 20,000 Companies, 1991. vol.1-5. Bristol: Jordan & Sons Ltd.

Block, P.M.(1987). 'Glasnost Eases the Way for Soviet Joint Venture', *Chemical Week*. vol.141 no.21. pp.32-6.

BNC (British-Nigeria Chamber of Commerce). A note presented at a seminar on 'Export Opportunities in the Agriculture Sectors in Nigeria and Kenya'. 29 November 1990. Department of Trade and Industry. London.

Brada, J.C.(1977). 'Markets, Property Rights, & the Economics of Joint Ventures in Socialist Countries', *Journal of Competitive Economics*. vol.1 part 2. pp.167-81.

Britains Top Privately Owned Companies, 1991. Vol. 1-5. Bristol: Jordan and Sons Ltd.

Cairns Holdings Ltd. *Annual Report 1990*. Harare.

Cavusgil, S.T. & Ghauri, P.N.(1990). *Doing Business in Developing Countries: Entry and Negotiation Strategies*. London: Routledge.

CCFT (1991). Cold Comfort Farm Trust: Development Programme, 1990 Annual Report and 1991 Plans. Harare. (unpublished monograph).

CDC (1991). 'Back to Office Report: RVDC, Zimbabwe. Review Mission 10-12 June, 1991'. July 1991. (unpublished report).

Chen, E.K.Y.(ed.) (1990). *Foreign Direct Investment in Asia.* Tokyo: Asia Productivity Organization.

Chernatony, L.de (1989). 'Achieving High Response Rates: a Survey of Postal Research', *Working Paper SWP9/89.* Cranfield: Cranfield School of Management.

_____, (1988). 'Getting the Most From Postal Research', *Working Paper SW23/88.* Cranfield: Cranfield School of Management.

Choudhury, M.A.J.(1989). *International Joint Ventures: Some Interfirm-Organization Specific Determinants of Successes and Failures: a Factor Analytic Exploration.* unpublished PhD Thesis. Temple University.

Cohen, J.A.(1982). 'Equity Joint Ventures: 20 Pitfalls that Every Company Shall Know About', *The China Business Review.* November-December. pp.26-30.

Commercial Agriculture in Zimbabwe, 1990/91. Harare: Modern Farming Publications. 1991.

'Companies with British Interests in African Countries 1990/91'. London: the Department of Trade and Industry (DTI). (unpublished document).

Connoly, S.G.(1984). 'Joint Ventures with Third World Multi-nationals: a New Form of Entry to International Markets', *Columbia Journal of World Business.* vol.19 no.2. pp.18-22.

'Council of State Special Decree No.11/1989'. *The Ethiopian Trade Journal.* 1989. vol.8 no.2-3. pp.35-42.

Cundiff, E.W. & Hilger, M.T.(1988). *Marketing in the International Environment.* 2nd Edition. Prentice-Hall Inc.

Davidson, W.H.(1982). *Global Strategic Management.* New York: John Wiley and Sons.

Dawson, L.M.(1987). 'Transferring Industrial Technology to Less Developed Countries', *Industrial Marketing Management.* vol.16 no.4. pp.265-71.

Dibb, D.N.(1987). 'H J Heinz in Zimbabwe', *Challenge.* January-February. vol.29 no.6. pp.32-6.

Dillon, W.R. et al.(1990). *Marketing Research in a Marketing Environment.* 2nd edition. Boston: Richard D Irwin, Inc.

Dinham, B. & Hines, C.(1983). *Agribusiness in Africa.* London: Earth Resources Research Ltd.

Directory 1991-92. London: British Consultants Bureau.

Dodwell, D.(1992). 'Investors Avoiding Cheap-labour States', *Financial Times.* May 21.

Dooley, D.(1984). *Social Research Methods.* New Jersey: Prentice-Hall.

Downey, W.D. & Erickson, S.P.(1987). *Agribusiness Management.* 2nd edition. McGraw-Hill.

Eales, R.(1990). 'Joint Ventures: Partners for Richer or Poorer', *The Independent on Sunday.* 18 March.

'Economics Brief: the Bleak Continent', *The Economist.* December 9, 1989.

Edris, T.A. & Meidan, A.(1990). 'On the Reliability of Psychographic Research: Encouraging Signs for Measurement Accuracy and Methodology in Consumer Research', *European Journal of Marketing.* vol.24 no.3. pp.23-41.

European Food Trades Directory 1991-92. Vol.1. United Kingdom. 22nd Edition. London: Newman Books Ltd.

Evans, M.(1990). 'MINITAB: A Guide to Survey Data Entry and Analysis', *Graduate Management Research.* vol.4 no.4. Spring. pp. 36-61.

Exporter List 1991, Series 2. East Africa. Southport: Freight Information Services Publications Ltd.

Exporter List 1991, Series 2. Nigeria and West Africa. Southport: Freight Information Services Publications Ltd.

FAME (Financial Analysis Made Easy): Database of Accounts of Major Public & Private British Companies. Version 4.2. London: Jordans & Sons. 1992.

Fieldman, G.M.(1987). 'US Trade Outlook: sub-Saharan Africa', *Business America.* vol.10 no.20. September 28. pp.21-5.

Fink, A. & Kosecoff, J.(1985). *How to Conduct Surveys: a Step-by-step Guide.* SAGE Publications.

Forrest, J.E.(1990). 'Strategic Alliances and Small Technology-Based Firm', *Journal of Small Business Management.* vol.28 no.3. pp.37-45.

Franko, L.G.(1987). 'New Forms of Investment in Developing Countries by US Companies: a Five Industries Comparison', *The Columbia Journal of World Business.* vol.22 no.2. pp.39-55.

Fraser, C. & Hite, R.E.(1988). 'Compensation as an Alternative to Ownership in Developing Markets: Beliefs, Attitudes and Uses', *Journal of World Trade.* vol.22 no.6. December. pp.95-106.

Freidmann, W.G. & Kalmanoff, G.(1961). *Joint International Business Ventures.* New York: Columbia University Press.

Gatlung, J.(1969). *Theory and Methods of Social Research.* New York: Columbia University Press.

George, S.(1977). *How the Other Half Dies: the Real Reasons for World Hunger*. Penguin Books.

Globerman, S.(1988). 'Government Policies Towards Foreign Direct Investment: Has a New Era Dawned?', *The Columbia Journal of World Business*. vol.23 no.3. pp.41-9.

Glover, D. & Kusterer, K.(1990). *Small Farmers, Big Business*. Houndmills: the MacMillan Press Ltd.

Goldenberg, S.(1989). *International Joint Ventures in Action*. Hutchinson Business Books.

Gomes-Casseres, B.(1987). 'Joint Venture Instability: Is it a Problem', *The Columbia Journal of World Business*. vol.22 no.2. pp.97-101.

Government of Zambia (1990). The Investment Act, 1990. Lusaka. (draft monograph).

Greene, J. and Villaneuva, D.(1990). 'Determinants of Private Investment in Less Developed Countries', *Finance & Development*. December. pp.40-2.

Gullander, S.(1976). 'Joint Ventures and Corporate Strategy', *Columbia Journal of World Business*. vol.11 no.1. Spring. pp.104-14.

_____, (1976). 'Joint Ventures in Europe: Determinants of Entry', *International Studies of Management and Organizations*. vol.1-2 no.6. Spring-Summer. pp.85-111.

Habib, G.M. & Burnett, J.J.(1989). 'An Assessment of Channel Behavior in an Alternative Structural Arrangement: the International Joint Venture', *International Marketing Review*. vol.6 no.3. pp.7-21.

Harrigan, K.R.(1988). 'Joint Ventures and Competitive Strategy', *Strategic Management Journal*. vol.9 no.2. pp.141-58.

_____, (1987). 'Strategic Alliances: Their New Role in Global Competition', *The Columbia Journal of World Business*. vol.22 no.2. pp.67-9.

_____, (1986). *Managing for Joint Venture Success*. Lexington: Heath & Co.

Harrison, J.S.(1987). 'Alternatives to Merger: Joint Ventures and Other Strategies', *Long Range Planning*. vol.20. no.6. pp.78-83.

Hertzfeld, J.M.(1991). 'Joint Ventures: Saving the Soviets From Perestroika', *Harvard Business Review*. January-February. pp.80-91.

Herzfeld, E.(1989). *Joint Ventures*. 2nd edition. Jordans.

Hewaidy, A.M.(1988). *Host Government Control of Foreign Manufacturing Companies: the Egyptian Experience*. unpublished PhD Thesis. University of East Anglia.

Hill, R.(1981). 'Are Multinationals Aliens in the Third World?', *International Management*. January. pp.12-16.

Hill, R.W. & Paliwoda, S.(1977). 'Poland Favors the Multinational', *Sales Engineering*. May. pp.2-5.

Holmes, C.(1974). 'A Statistical Evaluation of Rating Scales', *Journal of the Market Research Society*. Vol.16 no.2. pp.87-108.

Hosking, P.(1992). 'Sainsbury Profits from New Lines', *The Independent*. May 14.

Hunyani Holdings Ltd. *Annual Report 1990*. Harare.

IAD (1991). 'Sustainable Agriculture - What It Implies', *International Agricultural Development*. vol.11 no.3. May/June, 1991. Reading, UK.

IPC (Investment Promotion Centre) (1989). Investors' Guide to Kenya: Volume II. Nairobi.

Kay, N. et al. (1987). 'An Approach to the Analysis of Joint Ventures', *Working Paper No.87/313*. Florence: European University Institute .

Kent, D.H.(1991). 'Joint Ventures vs. Non-Joint Ventures: an Empirical Investigation', *Strategic Management Journal*. vol.12. pp.387-93.

Key British Enterprises 1992: Britain's Top 50,000 Companies. Vol. 1-6. High Wycombe: Dun & Bradstreet Ltd.

Killick, T.(1992). 'Explaining Africa's Post-Independence Development Experiences', *ODI Working Paper 60*. ODI: London.

Killing, J.P.(1983). *Strategies for Joint Venture Success*. Croom Helm Ltd.

_____(1980). 'Technology Acquisition: License Agreement or Joint Ventures', *The Columbia Journal of World Business*. Fall. pp.38-47. .

Knowles, L.L. and Mathur, I.(1989). 'Joint Venture Strategies for Marketing in China', *Journal of International Consumer Marketing*. vol.2 no.1. pp.37-54.

Kogut, B.(1988). 'Joint Ventures: Theoretical and Empirical Perspectives', *Strategic Management Journal*. vol.9. pp.319-32.

Kompass, United Kingdom 1991/92. Vol.II. Company Information. West Sussex: Reed Information Services Ltd.

Krausz, E. & Miller, S.H.(1974). *Social Research Design*. London: Longman Group Ltd.

Kristensen, E.(1987). 'Proof that a Joint Venture Can Work', *The Courier*. March-April. no.102. pp.98-9.

Kunjeku, P.F.(1991). *Project Finance and Technical Support Available to Zimbabwe*. Harare: Confederation of Zimbabwe Industries.

'Leading European and UK Companies', *Financial Times*. January 13, 1992. (Separate Section pp.27-31).

Linklaters & Paines and Nightingale, C.(1990). *Joint Ventures*. 1st edition. London: Longman Group UK Ltd.

Loutfi, M.(1989). 'Development Issues and State Policies in sub-Saharan Africa', *International Labor Review.* Vol.128 no.2. pp. 137-53.

M'baye, S.(1992). 'Rebuilding the Continent', *West Africa.* May 11-17.

Macleod, S. (ed) (1991). *The Directory of British Importers 1991. Vol. I & II.* Berkhamsted: Trade Research Publication.

Mashakada, T.(1991). 'What Unique Attributes Do We Have to Perform Wonders with ESAP', *The Financial Gazette*, August 22. Harare.

Max-Neef, M. et al.(1989). 'Development & Self-reliance', *Development Dialogue 1989:* 1. Uppsala: The Dag Hammerskjold Foundation.

Maya, S. & Tongoona, H.(1989). 'Ownership Structure of the Manufacturing Sector vol.II.' *Consultancy Report no.9.* Harare: Zimbabwe Institute of Development Studies .

McGee, J. & Segal-Horn, S.(1989). 'Changes in the European Food Processing Industry: the Consequences of 1992', *Working Paper SWP 29/89.* Cranfield: Cranfield School of Management.

Meadley, J.(1989). A More Significant Role for the Private Sector in Agricultural Development. (unpublished monograph).

Meddis, R.(1984). *Statistics Using Ranks: a Unified Approach.* Oxford: Basil Blackwell Publisher Ltd.

Meleka, A.H.(1985). 'The Changing Role of Multinational Corporations', *Management International Review.* vol.25 no.1. pp.36-45.

Mengistu, B. & Haile-Mariam, Y.(1988). 'The State & Future of Privatization in Sub-Saharan Africa', *Journal of African Studies*, vol.15 no.1&2. Spring/Summer. pp.4-9.

Miles, M.B. & Huberman, A.M.(1984). *Qualitative Data Analysis.* Beverly Hills: SAGE Publication Inc.

Miller, D.C.(1983). *Handbook of Research Design and Social Measurement.* 4th. ed. New York: Longman.

Montagnon, P.(1990). 'The Good and Bad News for Aid Recipients', *Financial Time.* December 6.

Morris, D. & Hergert, M.(1987). 'Trends in International Collaborative Agreements', *The Columbia Journal of World Business.* vol.22 no.2. pp.15-21.

Moyo, J.(1991). 'Economic Reform Programme is a Foreign Product', *The Financial Gazette*, September 5. Harare.

Najafbagy, R.(1985). 'Operations of Multinational Corporations and Local Enterprise in Arab Countries', *Management International Review.* vol.25 No.4. pp.46-57.

'Nigerian Companies in Joint Ventures'. *West Africa*. 1992. May 11-17.

Norusis, M.J.(1988). *SPSS/PC+ V2.0 Base Manual.* Chicago: SPSS, Inc.

Nuttall D.L.(1986). *Block 5: Classification and Measurement.* Milton Keynes: Open University Press.

O'Reilly, A.J.F.(1988). 'Establishing Successful Joint Ventures in Developing Countries: an CEO's Perspective', *The Columbia Journal of World Business.* Spring. vol.23. pp.65-71.

O'Sullivan, P. (1985). 'Determinants and Impact of Private Foreign Direct Investment in Host Countries', *Management International Review.* vol.25 no.1. pp.28-35.

Oates, D.(1986). 'Enterprise: the New China syndrome', *Director.* vol.40 no.3. October. pp.36-9.

Olivine Today, (3rd & 1st Quarters, 1991; 4th, 3rd, 2nd, & 1st Quarters, 1990). Harare.

Oman, C.(1989). *New Forms of Investment in Developing Country Industries.* Paris: OECD.

Onah, J.O.(1989). 'The Role of Multinational Companies in the Agricultural Development of Nigeria', *Journal of International Food and Agribusiness Marketing.* Vol.1 no.2. pp.63-84.

Paliwoda, S.J.(1986). *International Marketing.* London: Heinemann Professional Publishers.

_____, (1981). *Joint East West Marketing and Production Ventures.* Gower Publishing Co. Ltd

_____, (1975). *Changing Trends in Polish Trade.* unpublished MSc Dissertation. Bradford University.

Parkinson, J.M.(1985). 'Marketing in Lesser Developed Countries', *The Quarterly Review of Marketing.* vol.11 no.1. Autumn. pp.12-15.

Pfeffer, J. & Salancik, G.R.(1978). *The External Control of Organizations.* New York: Harper & Row.

Planning Commission (1990). National Investment Promotion Policy, Tanzania. Dar Es Salaam. (draft monograph).

Pollio, G. & Riemenschneiner, C.H.(1988). 'The Coming Third World Investment Revival', *Harvard Business Review.* March-April. vol.66 no.2. pp.114-24.

'Poor Man's Burden: A Survey of the Third World', *The Economist,* September 23 1989.

Porkess, R.(1988). *Dictionary of Statistics.* Glasgow: Collins.

Porter, M.(1992). 'Capital Disadvantage: America's Failing Capital Investment System', *Harvard Business Review.* vol.70 no.5. September/October. pp.65-82.

Poynter, T.A.(1982). 'Government Intervention in Less Developed Countries: the Experience of Multinational Companies', *Journal of International Business Studies.* Spring-Summer. pp.9-25.

'Profit Margins Unchanged and Return on Capital Down', *The Grocer.* November 9 1991. pp.34-6.

Raveed, S.R. & Renforth, W.(1983). 'Sate Enterprise-Multinational Corporation Joint Ventures: How Well Do They Meet Both Partners' Needs?', *Management International Review.* vol. 1 Part 1. pp.47-57.

Robbs, P.(1989). 'Privatisation in Africa: Neither Pox nor Panacea', *Development International.* March-April. pp.27-30.

Robson, C.(1985). *Experiment, Design, and Statistics in Psychology.* 2nd edition. Harmondsworth: Penguin Books Ltd.

Samuelson, R.J.(1989). 'Capitalism and Freedom', *Newsweek.* June 12.

Selassie, H.G. & Hill, R.W.(1993). 'Factors Determining Joint Venture Formation in the Agribusiness Sector in SSACs', *Journal of International Food and Agribusiness Marketing.* vol.5 no.1. pp.73-93.

Sethia, N.(1988). 'From Regulation to Innovation: Emerging Trends in India', *New Management.* vol.6 no.2. pp.32-6.

Shenkar, O.(1990). 'International Joint Ventures' Problems in China: Risks and Remedies', *Long Range Planning.* vol.23 no.3. pp.82-90.

Siegel, A.(1956). *Non-parametric Tests for the Behavioural Sciences.* New York: McGraw-Hill Book Company, Inc.

Simiar, F.(1983). 'Major Causes of JV Failures in the Middle East: the Case of Iran', *Management International Review.* pp.58-68.

Smith, C.H.(1987). *Negotiating and Managing Joint Ventures: Lessons from Practical Experience.* Geneva: International Labor Organization.

Smith, N.C.(1990). 'The Case Study: A Vital Yet Misunderstood Research Method for Management', *Graduate Management Research.* vol.4 no.4. pp.4-26.

Srivastava, U.K.(1989). 'Agro-processing Industries: Potential, Constraints, and Tasks Ahead', *Indian Journal of Agricultural Economics.* July-September. vol.6 no.3. pp.242-55.

Steel, G.D. & Torrie, J.H.(1980). *Principles and Procedures of Statistics: A Biometrical Approach.* 2nd. edition. Tokyo: McGraw-Hill Kogakusha, Ltd.

Stevens, S.S.(1946). 'On the Theory of Scales of Measurements. Science', vol. 103, pp. 677-80, in Nuttall D L (1986). *Block 5: Classification and Measurement.* Milton Keynes: Open University Press.

Stoever, W.A.(1989). 'Why State Corporations in Developing Countries Have Failed to Attract Foreign Investment', *International Marketing Review*. vol.6 no.3. pp.62-78.

Stopford, J.M.(1976). 'Changing Perspectives on Investment by British Manufacturing Multinationals', *Journal of International Business Studies*. vol.7 no.2. pp.15-27.

_____& Wells, L.T.(Jr.) (1972). *Managing the Multinational Enterprise.* New York: Basic Books.

Sudman, S. (1983) 'Applied Sampling', in Rossi, P H et al. (eds). *Handbook of Survey Research.* Orlando: Academic Press Inc.

Svetlicic, M. (1986). 'Investment Promotion Measures: Experience of Regional Regimes for Joint Ventures', Paper delivered at the Symposium on Selective preferential arrangements between developed and developing countries. November 28-30. Helsinki.

Tomlinson, J.W.C.(1970). *The Joint Venture Process in International Business: India & Pakistan.* Cambridge: MIT Press.

Torok, S.J. et al.(1991). 'Management Assistance Needs of Small Food and Kindred Products Processors', *Agribusiness.* Vol. 7 No.5. pp.447-61.

Tropical Growers Association (TGA): *Annual Report and Accounts 1989.* London 1990.

Tull, D.S. & Hawkins, D.I.(1984). *Marketing Research: Measurement and Method.* 3rd edition. Macmillan Publishing Company.

Tuttle, R. & Buchmiller, J.(1988). 'Mauritania's Marine Fisheries Offer Untapped Commercial Opportunities for US Business', *Business America.* vol.109 no.10. May 9. pp.39-40.

'Uganda Welcomes Investors' (1991). *Newsweek.* April 29. UN (1989). *Joint Ventures as a Form of International Economic Cooperation.* New York: Taylor & Francis.

UNCTC (1988). *Transnational Corporations in World Development.* New York: United Nations.

_____(1981). *Transnational Corporations in Food and Beverage Processing.* New York: United Nations.

UNIDO (1991). *Zimbabwe: Investment Guide, PTA.* (draft monograph).

_____(1989). *Agro-processing Overview. Program Development Support Unit (PDSU).* Winter Report, December. (unpublished monograph).

_____(1989). PTA: Investor's Guide. (monograph).

Walizer, M.H. & Wienir, P.L.(1978). *Research Methods and Analysis: Searching for Relationships.* New York: Harper & Row.

Weisberg, H.F. & Brown, B.D.(1977). *An Introduction to Survey Research & Data Analysis*. San Fransisco: W H Freeman & Co.

Who Owns Whom 1991: United Kingdom and Republic of Ireland: vol. 1 & 2. High Wycombe: Dun & Bradstreet Ltd.

Widstrand, C. & Amin, S.(1975) (ed.). *Multinational Firms in Africa.* Uppsala: Scandinavian Institute of African Studies.

Wilde, R.V.(1991). 'Address by the Director of ZIC and Deputy Governor of the Reserve Bank of Zimbabwe to the ZNCC 1991 Congress on 15 May 1991 at the Victoria Falls'. Harare. (monograph).

Williams, S. & Karen, R.(1985). *Agribusiness and the Small-scale Farmer.* Westview Press.

World Bank (1990). *World Development Report 1990*. New York: Oxford University Press.

_____(1988). *World Development Report 1988*. New York: Oxford University Press.

Wright, R.W. and Russel, C.S.(1975). 'Joint Ventures in Developing Countries: Realities and Responses', *Columbia Journal of World Business.* Summer. pp.74-80.

Yin, R.K.(1989). *Case Study Research: Design and Methods.* Applied social research methods series. vol.5. Newbury Park: SAGE Publications Inc.